T0017057

PSYCHIC POWERS

PSYCHIC POWERS

UNLOCK YOUR NATURAL INTUITION

SAHAR HUNEIDI-PALMER

SIRIUS

All images courtesy of Shutterstock.

SIRIUS

This edition published in 2022 by Sirius Publishing, a division of
Arcturus Publishing Limited,
26/27 Bickels Yard, 151–153 Bermondsey Street,
London SE1 3HA

ISBN: 978-1-3988-2095-1
AD008728UK

Printed in China

Contents

INTRODUCTION

H istory is replete with accounts of the human desire to seek the unknown, beyond what could be perceived physically, in order to connect with what was beyond the physical senses, or 'para normal'. Foreseeing the future is as intriguing as the people who claim to have special powers, or who are psychics.

At least 5,000 years have elapsed since the first attempts to speak with the dead or make future prophecies. For example, the Ancient Egyptians used 'scrying' to read patterns created by dropping ink into water. The Mesopotamians did the same with oil. Moreover, Emperor Shennong Yan, who was recognized as the first Emperor of Ancient China, devised not just farming implements for his people, but also plants for curing their maladies. When he discovered tea as a beverage in 2737 BC, his subjects began reading tea leaves.

As Dutch merchants introduced tea to Europe via trade routes to China, tea-leaf reading became all the rage in Europe – especially in Victorian England. About a hundred years later, when the Ottoman Empire – which brought coffee to Europe via the Middle East – crumbled, this ritual evolved into coffee-cup reading. The Ottomans left Europe in a hurry, leaving behind sacks of coffee beans! Until then, the export of the miracle beans was outlawed, and coffee consumption was restricted to Arabia.

Coffee-cup readers became known as 'soothsayers' in Europe, persons who could soothe the spirit by giving good counsel or forecasting the future. The practice of reading tea leaves or coffee grounds became known as tasseography. This was a method of forecasting or getting insight into a person's personality, past and future. The name tasseography is derived from the French word 'tasse', which means cup, and the Arabic word 'graph', which means writing. Soothsayer is derived from the Old English word for 'truth' mixed with 'say', which means 'an act of speaking the truth'.

Today, many of us are familiar with tarot-card reading – another method of peering beyond normal perceptions of life, seeking insights and advice. The tarot, too, originated in Ancient China in the 9th century ad. The deck of cards was used as a betting tricks game to entertain the royal family of the Tang Dynasty. The card game spread with popularity throughout Asia and then into Egypt and through The Levant into Europe. Over time, it transformed into the divination cards we know as the Tarot, in the mid 15th century. By the time Nostradamus published *Les Prophéties* (The Prophecies) in 1555, he had already become the most famous soothsayer of all time, making global predictions for the ages. Rasputin, the renowned Russian mystic, enthralled his country – and, more importantly, the Russian rulers – in the first part of the twentieth century. And in Victorian England, occultism, spiritualism, and mediumship were popular – as were table turning (the lifting or manipulation of a table during a séance, attributed to spirits), séances (a meeting at which people attempt to contact the dead, especially through a medium) and flower readings.

No matter how far a culture or science has evolved, humanity's interest in the paranormal and psychics with extraordinary abilities continues unabated. According to a 2016 estimate, the psychic industry has risen fast since 2010, generating an estimated $2 billion in annual revenue. However, the question remains: what does it mean to be psychic? Another tantalizing question is whether anyone can develop psychic or intuitive talents. I hope that this book will inspire you to find more about what psychic abilities are, how they work, and how to develop your own through various tips and exercises.

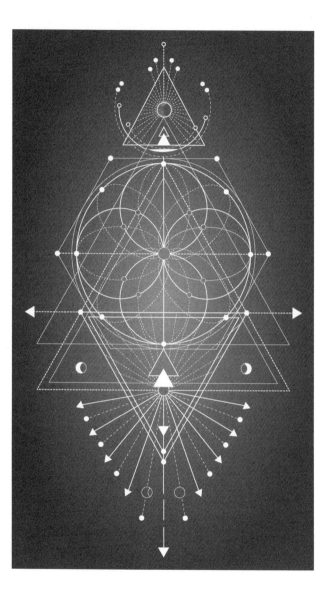

DEMYSTIFYING PSYCHIC POWERS

'*The Brain–is wider than the Sky–*
For–put them side by side–
The one the other will contain
With ease–and you–beside–'

EMILY DICKINSON, AMERICAN POET

Psychic power is a natural, built-in ability, or innate gift, that all human beings have. In the past, before it was understood, it was perceived as a 'power' or gift that few people were endowed with. Now, with advancements in science and the development of machines, we are able to measure the human energy field (aura) and scan brain activity. The abilities we call 'psychic powers' can be detected, measured and are now understood better, as you shall discover.

Many people are naturally psychic, or aware of their ability to sense things that we couldn't rationally know. The extra-sensory nature of this ability is the reason it was referred to as a gift. However, with practice and some understanding of what psychic perception is, you too can develop these abilities.

Think of psychic perception as your inner perception. It is an extension of the abilities of both the human body and the brain. Both body and brain can perceive information from the outer world around you through interacting with it. You do this naturally, every day, as you live your life.

During your daily life, you perform various activities which are fed as information to your brain. This information is picked through your conventional five senses. As a result, depending on the level of focus you require to perform these activates, your brain emanates brainwaves that have varying functions and abilities to help you cope and process this information more efficiently – as you will find out next.

This is how information is picked up and processed: your body, through your neuro-cellular (nerves) network, sends electrical signals to the brain. The brain then interprets these messages and helps you cope with each activity you are performing accordingly. In other words, your built-in senses help you perceive your surroundings, and your brain helps you navigate safely on a daily basis in order to survive.

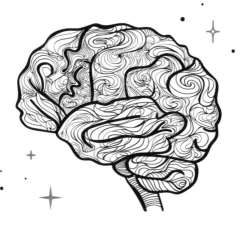

Your Outer Senses

You already sense your environment by gathering information using what is referred to as 'outer senses'. These are the five conventional senses that operate via visible or tangible means. Scientists, however, have now defined more than five senses. Noticing all you can with your conventional senses can help you develop your psychic sense, or your inner senses, within you. This is because your brain receives all information as electrical activity. All information is processed by your brain in the same way, however, on different levels of brainwave activity.

A *Scientific American* article published on December 22, 1997, entitled *What is the function of the various brainwaves?* states the following: "It is well known that the brain is an electrochemical organ." The scope of the human brain's function and ability varies according to activities we engage with. The various activities we engage in generate different electrical waves that emanate from your brain and are detected as waves. Brain activity can be detected and brainwave length can be measured.

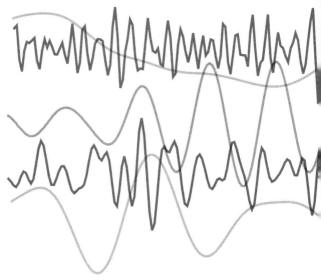

Brainwaves range from the most active state to the least. Each level of category of brainwaves, or range of frequencies, is associated with a different activity or function (see Table 1 on pages 18 and 19). Brain frequencies range from strongly engaged mind in problem-solving, for example, to deeply relaxed or non-aroused, to in deep sleep. Each range of waves

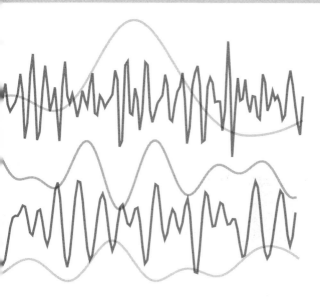

helps the brain function better in dealing with the information it senses or perceives. For example, when the brain is aroused and is actively engaged in mental activity, the displayed brainwave is Beta. There are four main categories of brainwaves that all human beings, including women, men and children, regardless of ethnicity or culture, experience and exhibit.

TABLE 1: TYPES OF BRAINWAVES

Gamma waves: 40 to 100 Hz	Gamma waves process information from various brain areas, conscious perception, high focus and concentration, learning.
Beta waves: 12 to 40 Hz. These are the most common daytime brainwaves.	Beta waves are dominant in normal wakeful states, and when you're focused on cognitive tasks such as problem-solving or decision-making.
Alpha waves: 8 to 12 Hz	Alpha waves are involved in how we think, feel, communicate, sleep and generally function.
Theta waves: 4 to 8 Hz	Theta waves also occur during sleep, and in very deep states of meditation.
Delta waves: 0.5 to 4 Hz	Delta waves are the slowest brainwaves, and occur in the deepest states of sleep.

LEVEL OF
BRAIN
ACTIVITY

These are the fastest of the brainwaves. Highly focused.
- Cognitive enhancement
- Attention to detail, aids memory recall
- Encourages a different way of thinking, which is a sign of creativity

Awake, focused, daily activity, attention; anxiety (higher 22Hz).
- Focused attention
- Solving problems
- Stimulates action
- High-level cognition

Very relaxed, awake, passive attention.
- Reduces stress
- Encourages positive thinking
- Increased learning abilities
- Engagement with environment, feeling in the flow

- Deep relaxation
- Meditation
- Creativity

- Deep sleep
- Healing & pain relief
- Meditation
- Anti-ageing: decreases cortisol/increases DHEA
- Accessing the unconscious

Brainwaves and Activity

Brainwaves are evidence of electrical activity in your brain. When one group of neurons sends a burst of electrical pulses to another group of neurons, a wave-like pattern is formed. Your brain is constantly at work, performing functions such as thinking, concentrating, remembering, and so on. During these actions, your brain cells are constantly talking with one another.

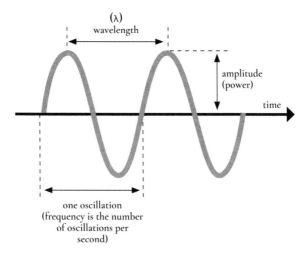

FIGURE 1 Brainwave frequency and amplitude

Brainwaves are the patterns or rhythms that come from this. These brainwave states range from deep, dreamless sleep to ecstasy. This means your brainwaves can be both fast and slow. Fast brainwaves have low magnitude, or power, known as amplitude. And slower brainwaves have larger amplitude.

The speed of brainwaves is referred to as frequency, and is expressed in cycles per second (which is measured in Hertz; see Table 1). According to researchers, a fully functional brain can create up to 10 watts of electrical power. When you are awake and attentive, your brain is more active. This results in fast brainwaves. If you are sleepy or bored, they may be slower. When brainwaves are fast, they have low amplitude. And, when brainwaves are slower, they have higher amplitude (see Figure 1).

Moreover, brainwaves are measured using Electro-encephalography (EEG) and magnetoencephalography (MEG). The procedure entails placing electrodes or sensors onto your head to measure brain activity. All humans have the same four brainwave states. Men, women, and children of all ages experience the same characteristic brainwaves.

Brainwaves are universal beyond cultures and national boundaries. When you are aware of the brain's various functions, or wave states, you can train yourself to be in a wave state. For example, by concentrating and slowing your breathing, your brain's activity level lessens, which helps you get into a meditative state, such as alpha, and tune in to your psychic ability, or a further theta for emotional healing, recalling memories and gaining insights, or inducing dreams when you train yourself to reach delta!

GAMMA STATE

The fastest brain-activity range is gamma waves, which indicate peak concentration. When you are intently concentrating and actively engaged in problem-solving, your brain is likely producing gamma waves. Gamma brainwaves, which are difficult to measure with current equipment, show that your brain is actively digesting information and seeking solutions.

Meditation, according to research published by the National Institutes of Health in 2017, may help you produce more gamma waves. This is also the case with using Binaural beats or concentrating on your breathing. In fact, one yoga study found that participants who focused on their breath produced more gamma waves than those who focused on meditation.

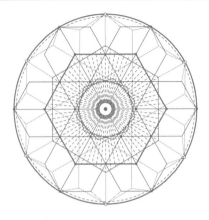

However, meditation methods vary widely. So, depending on what style of mediation you are practicing and the methods or rhythms of breathing you follow, different techniques may help achieve various results. The best method to find out which meditation style and brainwave state benefit you most is to track your progress and your experiences by starting a psychic-development journal. It is worth mentioning here that meditation has many other health benefits besides psychic skills. It has been demonstrated to help reduce stress, anxiety and depression too.

BETA STATE

The brain generates beta waves when it is stimulated and mentally busy. You are wide awake, attentive and concentrated when you have these brainwaves. You are typically going about your everyday routines and making decisions. This is when your brain produces beta waves that range between 12 and 40 Hz. Beta waves indicate a focused mind. When you are having a conversation, your brain will be in beta. If you are engaged in a debate, for instance, your beta waves would be high beta. A teacher or a TV talk-show host would be in beta too, when they are working.

ALPHA STATE

Alpha is the next brainwave frequency category. Whereas beta reflects arousal, alpha does not. When you are not focused hard on anything in particular, your brain produces these waves. Whatever you're doing, you're probably feeling relatively calm and relaxed.

Alpha brainwaves are slower and have larger amplitude. Their rate is 9–14 cycles per second. For instance, when you sit down to rest after finishing a task, you would be in an alpha state. Or, if you reflect or mediate regularly, you would generally be in an alpha state. For example, when you break away from a task or a meeting to walk in the garden, you would be in an alpha state. In other words, when you stop focusing on a task and try to relax and unwind, your brain may produce more alpha waves.

THETA STATE

When you are entirely relaxed or sleeping lightly, your brain may produce more theta waves. Theta brainwaves have a greater amplitude and a slower frequency than alpha brainwaves. Typically, this ranges between five and eight cycles per second. Theta state is induced by tasks that become so automatic that you may consciously disengage from them. People who drive on the highway, for example, are frequently inspired with fresh ideas when in theta.

A theta state occurs when a person is unable to recall the previous five miles while driving on a freeway. The repetitive nature of such driving, as opposed to driving on a country road, would separate a theta state from a beta state. Outdoor runners frequently enter theta, a slower-than-alpha phase of mental relaxation conducive

to creative thought. This could occur while shaving or brushing your hair. Also, when you take a break from work and start daydreaming, you are entering theta state. Inspiration is often free flowing in theta states, with no filtering or reluctance. It is generally being in a really good mood.

DELTA STATE

Delta is the final brainwave. Your brain produces delta waves, the slowest type of brainwave, when you are in a dreamless state of sleep. These brainwaves are strongest and slowest here. They usually range from 1.5 to 4 cycles per second. They never go to zero, because that would be brain death. But deep, dreamless sleep would lower your frequency to two to three cycles per second. We are in low beta when we read before bedtime. When

we put down the book, turn down the lights, and close our eyes, our brainwaves shift from beta to alpha, then theta, and eventually delta.

In summary, your brain does not stop producing one type of brainwave just because you change your level of consciousness or attention. Whether you are aware of it or not, there is always some type of electrical activity going on in your brain. Depending on what you are doing, one sort of electrical wave in your brain will dominate at different times of the day.

It is more likely that one form of brainwave will predominate at any particular time, depending on whether you're awake or sleeping, concentrating or drifting. If, however, your brain is not producing a lot of alpha waves, it indicates that you are not in a relaxed, meditative frame of mind. However, if you put your mind to it, you may be able to increase your alpha brainwaves, relax and activate your psychic abilities.

Paranormal Perception

Psychic, or what is referred to sometimes as paranormal (beyond normal) perception, is possible when the brain activity is in lower wavelength – that is, when you are relaxed. One of the best ways to start developing your psychic perception is to relax your mind through practicing breathing techniques, meditation or creative activity that encourages imagination, such as guided meditation or art (more on that in Chapter Four).

If you like, higher wave amplitudes have more 'power' to sense, or perceive, input your brain receives through your 'inner senses'. The brain's ability for higher perception and accelerated learning, for example, seems to be possible and is enhanced when it is in alpha wave (8–12 Hz, cycles per second).

José Silva, who started out as an electronics repairman in the US, was one of the earliest researchers into the brain's activity and related sensory perception abilities in the twentieth century. He wanted to see if he could help his children increase their IQ and enhance their intuition. He found out that an alpha state, when a person is relaxed yet aware, allows for accelerated learning, creativity, intuition and memory.

Independent scientific studies published in a report, *How science discovered the Silva method*, revealed his pioneering research, and how he gained the approval of the scientific community. The eye-opening studies that support his findings have since demonstrated that alpha brainwave activity is associated with inner levels of mental activity. To put it simply, when you are relaxed but awake, your brain activity is on a certain wavelength that allows the brain to perceive more information.

José Silva (1914 – 1999)

Silva joined the Signal Corps during WWII and was checked by an Army psychiatrist after his induction. Silva, intrigued by the psychiatrist's peculiar queries, enquired about a hypnosis book in the psychiatrist's library. As a result, Silva became interested in psychology, specifically the nature of hypnotic suggestion and perception in altered states. He studied advanced electronics and became an instructor while serving in the Signal Corps. During the 1940s, he devised a set of tactics with the goal of altering his children's IQs and developing their psychic powers (e.g. clairvoyance).

His experiments were based on his background in electronics and his interest in psychology. He'd read about alpha waves and electrical activity in the human brain and had purchased an electroencephalograph (EEG). EEG is a method used to measure the electrical activity of the brain by tracking and recording brainwave patterns. Small metal discs with thin wires (electrodes) are placed on the scalp, and these send signals to a computer to record the results.

He discovered that one portion of the brain, the one that generates alpha brainwave activity, was more powerful than the others. This told him that the electrical impedance (the opposition to electrical flow) of this part of the brain was lower, so it would work more efficiently. Silva reasoned that because this region of the brain worked more efficiently, it could receive and store more information.

Silva experimented with hypnosis but he concluded that, while hypnosis made the mind more responsive, greater individual control was required for improved brain function. He next experimented with mental training techniques to quiet the brain while keeping it more awake than in hypnosis. This, he reasoned, would result in greater memory and comprehension, and so higher IQ ratings. Silva's approaches grew from workouts that required relaxed attention, vivid mental vision and methods of reaching lesser levels. He considered that these levels were more successful than the fully awake, or beta wave (12.5 and 30 Hz, cycles per second), level in terms of learning. Silva's proof was that throughout the three years he worked with his children to test his theories, their grades in school significantly improved.

In 1944 Silva began developing The Silva Method, formerly known as Silva Mind Control. He created a curriculum that taught people how to access various brain states of improved awareness. He also created a number of systematic mental procedures to be used when in these states, allowing a person to mentally project with a specified aim. Silva claims that after

the mind is projected, a person can see distant objects or locations and communicate with higher intellect for advice. The information received by the projected mind is stated to be perceived by the mind as thoughts, images, feelings, smells, taste and sound. The data gathered in this manner can be used to solve problems.

In 1960, Silva launched his method, teaching it to the public to help them develop better mind abilities. A *New York Times* article on April 16, 1972 (*Can Man Control His Mind?*) reported that a Trinity University study showed that students trained in Mind Control did attain a high degree of alpha level production. It also noted that C. W. Post College and Canisius College would offer courses in Silva's methods. Silva died peacefully in February 1999, aged 84. The Silva Ultra Mind ESP System was his final creation, and was completed shortly before he died.

Outer Sensing, Inner Sensing and Perception

Simply put, Extra Sensory Perception is an ability of the brain to perceive with our inner senses when it is in alpha state or beta wavelength state. Your inner senses are similar to the outer senses; however, inner senses perceive information through the mind, without physical contact. Your brain then interprets that information through the sense of taste, touch, vision, smell or hearing. Our outer senses are the means by which we perceive the physical world around us. These are:

- **Sight (vision):**
  The eyes translate light into image signals for the brain to process.

- **Hearing (auditory):**
  The ear uses bones and fluid to transform sound waves into sound signals.

- **Smell (olfactory):**
  Chemicals in the air
  stimulate signals that the
  brain interprets as smells.

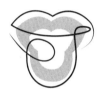

- **Taste (gustatory):**
  Food particles are sensed
  by receptor proteins on
  the taste bud cells, which
  signal the brain.

- **Touch (tactile):**
  Specialized receptors
  in the skin send touch
  signals to the brain.

With practice, you can activate your inner senses. So, sight becomes clairvoyance, which is the ability to perceive visually with the inner senses. Hearing with our inner ears is known as clairaudience. You will get to know your inner senses in the following chapter.

Additionally, we have two other senses that help us navigate our environment:

• **Vestibular** (movement): The movement and balance sense, which tells us where our head and body are in space, assists us in remaining upright while we sit, stand or walk.

• **Proprioception** (body position): Sensation-based awareness of one's posture, movement, balance, and location. To put it another way, knowing which portions of your body are where without having to look. It's how we can type without looking at the keyboard, or walk around without looking at our feet.

Fundamentally, you gather information through your main physical senses, which then feed the data or information to your brain. This information is then interpreted by your brain. The brain then makes sense of this information based on your prior experience (and subsequent learning), as well as the combination of information from each sense.

Most sensory input elicits an automatic response. This is how our brain helps us 'survive'. Such a reaction is critical to sustain us in our environment. Neuroscientists understand that human beings are a collection of senses. Many believe that we have between 22 and 33 separate senses! Here are a few of the less well-known ones:

- **Equilibrioception:** A sense of balance. This is what keeps us upright and helps us make our way around without getting hurt.

- **Kinaesthesia:** The ability to sense the position and movement of our limbs and trunk.

- **Thermoception:** The ability to sense temperature, whether our environment is too cold or too hot. It helps keep us alive and well.

- **Nociception:** The ability to feel pain.

- **Chronoception**: How we sense the passing of time.

Moreover, there are also some senses that are only found in the animal world:

- **Electroception**: The ability to detect electrical fields in our surroundings. Sharks can detect electrical fields in their surroundings, including those created by prey that they cannot see.

- **Magnetoreception**: Some mammals, including bats, can detect and use the Earth's magnetic field to navigate.

As the above list suggests, you have more ways of perceiving than just through the known conventional five senses. As humans, we experience **multisensory** perception. This means that all of your senses work together to provide you with a complete picture of your environment, and your body, which is **not** limited to what each sense perceives separately.

The five senses operate together to present the brain with a more complete picture, which allows it to respond appropriately. What one sense perceives can affect what another sense perceives too. All your senses work together to help your brain perceive an overall and complete picture.

Moreover, you have sensors all over your body that detect different types of information. Just as your eyes detect light, you have sensors all over your skin that detect pressure, as well as other sensors that detect pain. All these different sensors are neurons that specialize in picking up, or detecting, different types of information. And when they do, these specialized sensors generate an electrical impulse that is transmitted through a neuronal fibre, bundled in a nerve, all the way to the central nervous system. This happens extremely fast.

In the central nervous system, you have specialized groups of different neurons to process the information and generate the appropriate responses. The remarkable thing about your nervous system is that it does these types of processes on all types of information all of the time. And, in addition to gathering information from the outside environment, it gathers information from within you, such as muscle activity, respiration, stomach activity and so on. And it can handle all of them at the same time! As a result, it enables you to respond to and communicate with the environment around you in the most effective manner imaginable.

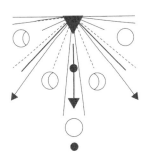

Pre-Feeling

You are also able to perceive through your inner senses, even without looking! Hilary Hurd Anyaso, Senior Managing Editor of *Northwestern Now*, wrote in her article *Can Your Body Sense Future Events Without Any External Clue?* (published in October 22, 2012): 'Researchers already know that our subconscious minds sometimes know more than our conscious minds.' According to new published research by Northwestern University, scientists who analyzed 26 studies conducted between 1978 and 2010 suggest that, "If you were tuned into your body, you might be able to detect these anticipatory changes between two and 10 seconds beforehand." Scientists called this ability 'pre-feelings' or 'pre-sentiment', which is the ability to anticipate the near future.

Scientist Mossbridge adds, "We can't explain it using present-day understanding about how biology works, though explanations related to recent quantum biological findings could potentially make sense. It's anticipatory because it seems to predict future physiological changes in response to an important event without any known clues, and it's an activity because it consists of changes in the cardiopulmonary, skin and nervous systems."

For instance, when you are sitting at a desk in a library or a café, engaged in a book you are reading or working on your laptop, you can feel or sense if someone behind you is staring at you. In an altered state, or a meditative state, our senses work on a deeper level, and our mind allows us to perceive time, objects or an environment that we are not physically or directly in touch with. For instance, while you are sleeping, you have what appears to be a long and complex dream with vivid events that appear to be real. When you wake up, you realize you have only slept for ten minutes! In that state, your view of time changes, and perception of reality shifts. "The cause of this anticipatory activity," adds Mossbridge, "which undoubtedly lies within the realm of natural physical processes (as opposed to supernatural or paranormal ones), remains to be determined."

To summarize, your brain, through your body's outer and inner senses, is always processing information. All the senses work together to build a picture of

what you are perceiving. When you are aware of what you are sensing through the conventional senses, it will strengthen your awareness to perceive subtle information psychically.

In addition, when you train yourself to relax, your brain switches to a dominant state, such as alpha, which allows for psychic perception. In the next chapter, we will discuss how psychic perception happens, how time is perceived, and the various psychic abilities. Have confidence in yourself, knowing that you can *already* do this!

CHAPTER TWO

PSYCHIC PERCEPTION

'*I shall not commit the fashionable
stupidity of regarding everything
I cannot explain as a fraud.*'

C.G. JUNG

Your inner senses also help you receive intuitive information. This can happen even when you are not awake, such as when you are sleeping, through your dreams. For example, in your sleep, you might dream that you are running and feel thirsty. You might wake up just to have a drink of water. In a way, your inner senses correspond to your outer conventional senses and receive information in a similar way, when you are in an 'alerted state' – or a slower brainwave state. In an altered, or meditative, state, your senses and mind function on a deeper level. This allows you to perceive time, objects, an environment or a location with which you are not physically or directly in touch.

Sleep state is a great example of when and how this happens! While sleeping, you may experience what appears to be a long and intricate dream that seems to be detailed and real – perhaps even of a place where you have never been. However, upon waking up, you realize that you have only slept for ten minutes and that you are still in the same place you went to sleep in – and not connected to the location where the dream took place. Your brain is still receiving and processing information. However, in that altered state, your perception of time and space has changed, and so did your experience of what is real.

Psychic perception starts with sensing the world through the main conventional physical senses. The main senses are the means through which information is picked up and is delivered to your brain. The more aware you are of what you are sensing during your daily life, the stronger your psychic perception will become. You have already learned how your perception changes based on your level of consciousness or focus.

To help you perceive information, your brain creates electrical waves such as alpha, theta and delta, which alter in frequency and amplitude. When you are actively engaged in tasks that require your attention, your brain produces higher-frequency waves to help stay alert. Lesser-frequency brainwaves, however, have more amplitude, or power, allowing your brain to perceive subtle information as you relax. This increases your awareness and ability to perceive information outside of your usual range of perception. You feel motivated and inspired, and your creativity flows.

As your consciousness shifts, psychic perception, or intuition, becomes possible. So, when you are calm or resting, your attention is needed to focus on physical reality. As your brainwaves change to lesser frequencies, but higher amplitude, your consciousness expands to a higher level where your brain can perceive subtle information.

Perception of Time

The dimension of time seems to be mysterious. Understanding how your mind perceives time will help you make sense of the information you receive through your inner senses – for example, whether you are perceiving information about the past, the present or the future.

Your perception of time also changes according to your awareness level and brainwaves. When you develop your psychic abilities and start perceiving information through your inner senses, gaining an understanding of how your perception of time changes will help you make sense of the information you receive.

There is no one specific part of the brain that deals with time. "The interesting thing about time," says David Eagleman, a neuroscientist at Baylor College of Medicine, in Houston, "is it's a distributed property. It's **metasensory**; it rides on top of all the others...". (*Meta* is a word derived from the Greek language, and means 'beyond' or 'transcending'.)

That metasensory process influences the perception of time; when we are bombarded with fresh information, it takes our brains some time to grasp it all. The longer this processing takes, the longer that time feels. What

is even stranger is how the brain coordinates all the information it receives. For example, when you are doing anything (or a number of things) for the first time, the task requires your whole attention. The curious thing is that by concentrating on what you were doing, you really slow down time (or how your brain perceived that time, anyway). In contrast, when you are having fun and enjoying yourself, time seems to fly by quickly.

In an interview in the *New York Times* in 2011, *The Possibilian: What a brush with death taught David Eagleman*, Eagleman says that 'brain time' is intrinsically subjective. "Try this exercise," he suggests. "Put this book down and go look in a mirror. Now move your eyes back and forth, so that you're looking at your left eye, then at your right eye, then at your left eye again. When your eyes shift from one position to the other, they take time to move and land on the other location. But here's the kicker: you never see your eyes move. Where did the missing moments go?" Effectively, your brain has simplified a complex scenario of eyeballs darting back and forth into a simple one: your eyes look straight ahead.

Linear Time and Circular Time

We are all affected by the passing of time. One fact is certain: you can never be ahead or behind it. Your physical body, for example, cannot travel back in time and appear younger than it is now, as it did, say 10 years ago. Time is linear for such well-defined physical things. A fully grown tree that has been chopped cannot be restored. There is a beginning and an end to everything.

In other words, your physical body is the reference point to what you perceive in this moment that you are living right now. When our awareness is on the body and mind, such as when you are going about your usual day, time becomes a linear dimension. Your brain requires this to enable you to cope on a daily basis. In this sense, the past and future are imaginary – yet you can recall the past, and dream about, or project your thoughts into, the future.

LINEAR TIME

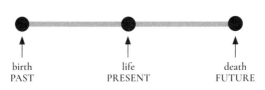

birth
PAST

life
PRESENT

death
FUTURE

CIRCULAR TIME

BEGINNING
& END

FIGURE 2 Perception of time

However, the way your body changes in appearance as you age demonstrates the effect of time. In that sense, too, time is a linear quality. It marks birth (past), life (present) and death (future), or yesterday, today and tomorrow. As you go about your day, your brain perceives time in a linear way to be able to cope and plan.

In alert states of awareness, however, time appears to contract or stretch, as explained earlier. In other words, your perception of time changes when your brainwaves change as you relax, or when you do not need to be focused and alert. In that state, your perception of time can be described as 'circular'.

"In Western philosophy, the concept of linear time is dominant," says Dr. Niranjan Seshadri, a cardiologist at Hays Medical Center in Kansas, USA. "On the other hand, Eastern philosophies see time as cyclical or circular like a wheel...This wheel of time is in continual motion... From the perspective of the body, which does not usually live beyond tens of decades, such time scales, which run into thousands of years, carry little meaning. But, from the perspective of mental evolution, transformation can happen within one's lifetime."

Dr. Seshadri suggests that "We can divide the mind into four parts – the unconscious, the subconscious, the conscious, and the superconscious." The unconscious corresponds to the deep, dreamless state of sleep, the subconscious corresponds to the dream state of sleep and the conscious corresponds to the ordinary waking state. The superconscious mind refers to when "awareness can remain independent of these three states." Keep in mind that you switch cyclically between these phases each day and night. In effect, when time moves through these three states of wakefulness, dream, and deep sleep states, it becomes a circular dimension. In other words, we cannot say which is the beginning and which the end (see Figure 2).

Time Travel

Understanding how your brain perceives time will help
you become aware of what happens in meditations
or visualizations. When you practice visualization
with the intention of manifesting future goals, you
are programming or projecting your thoughts in time

towards what you would like to happen in the future.
You are visualizing in circular time, if you like, and
your body is not a reference point, since this would be
a mental exercise. Since time is only perceived as linear
in a fully awake state, in a meditative state you are
'visiting' your future with your mind and programming
your goals to manifest. In a sense, you are travelling to
future time.

Similarly, time travel through a visualization can help
you reprogram, or change, the past in order to create a
better outcome or a happier future. Recalling a painful
incident from the past, for instance, may bring up the
same emotional responses you had at that point in the
past. Although you cognitively know that the memory
took place in the past, your brain is experiencing it as
though it is happening again – now.

You may even have bodily reactions as you recall it.
And, if the trauma is deep-seated, it might build
a mental block that prevents you from seeing a
different future because it seems logically impossible
to your brain. Your mind effectively believes 'since a
previous event was so horrible, and I'm still feeling the

consequences in the present, how can the future be different?'

This is actually how the brain works. It learns from your past, from what was a painful or threatening situation, and stops you form repeating it – unbeknown to you. When you develop your self-awareness, such issues will come into the light. Rewriting the past will make it possible for your brain to perceive a different outcome to the negative experience you went through, such as a painful breakup of a relationship, or being abandoned as a child and still feeling unsupported or uncared for. Using your psychic skills, and inner abilities such as imagination, creativity and inner senses, you can use visualization techniques to travel backward and forward in time. See the Rewriting the Past visualization technique below.

The following figure helps to demonstrate the concept of circular time:

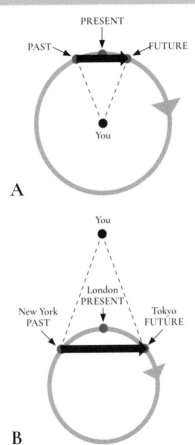

FIGURE 3 *Perception of circular & linear time*

If you were standing in the centre of the circular time wheel, in Figure 3 A, you would be living in the present, and your brain would see time as linear: past, present and future. This is symbolized by an arrow pointing from left to right, past to future. To further understand the circular time concept, suppose you are in a satellite hovering over London at midnight local time, and staring down at planet earth. Tokyo would have already begun their tomorrow, whilst London might just be finishing today and New York would still be in yesterday's time!

Your brain is already equipped to deal with the illusion of time, and it may even work to your advantage. You can use your imagination and this concept to visualize changing a negative occurrence or belief from the past, which will change how you perceive your present and allow your mind to perceive a new and more optimistic outcome in the future. By altering a past memory, you alter your perception of how you perceive it, and your mind becomes more receptive of a new future.

Your brain does not distinguish between what has actually occurred and what you believe has occurred.

Nor does it distinguish between what you believe will happen and what you wish to happen in the future. It reacts and responds to your current feelings, ideas and impressions. This can be a blessing! Visualizations work because, to your brain, what you are feeling NOW is real.

As you think about moving on, please remember the following about your brain:

• Thoughts you experience in the present are what count.

• The brain reacts to what you perceive right now (not to what has happened).

• You can rewrite the past by changing your perception of it.

• Your linear mind is more likely to move forward once it perceives a different past.

• Don't analyze, visualize.

Rewriting the Past
VISUALIZATION TECHNIQUE

You can use this exercise to forgive yourself and others, for example. Rewriting the past enables you to move forward and create a brighter future.

1 Find a quiet spot where you can sit comfortably, relax and close your eyes. Take three deep breaths, holding in your breath each time for a few seconds; then expel all of your anxieties, leaving them behind.

2 Imagine that you are seated on a tree trunk, with a bright yellow-orange sun shining over your head. Get a sense of the bottom of your spine and mentally follow the golden rays of the sun from the top of your head into the tree trunk, and deep down to the roots of the tree, into the earth.

3 Allow your body to feel heavier and more comfortable as you exhale, knowing you are safe and anchored.

4 Clear your thoughts by focusing your attention on your head. Then, ask your mind what circumstance you need to rewrite. Allow a response to come to you naturally; it may not be what you expect. Now, visualize or bring up a memory of what has happened and how you feel about it.

5 This is your second chance. Begin reimagining the event by visualizing it unfolding the way you want it to, developing a new screenplay and feelings. See and hear other individuals who were involved respond positively to what is going on right now.

6 Allow yourself plenty of time. The success of 'rewriting' is determined by how authentic and real you make this visualization, so engage all your senses. Include details, senses, sounds and smells. Repeat, and repeat the visualization approach as needed. These are the new experiences.

7 Imagine that you ease as you and others involved reach an agreement. As your visualization ends, see yourself smiling and content.

8 When you feel that this outcome has been achieved, focus on the tree trunk you are sitting on, then the room you are in. Next, wiggle your toes, open your eyes and slowly stand up. Feel ecstatic about the new future that is now possible!

Sit back, smile, and look forward to a brighter future!

Types of Psychic Abilities

Intuition is defined as cognition, or knowing, that occurs without the use of conscious, rational thought processes. Having psychic ability explains the process of perceiving intuitive information. Although one psychic ability may be dominant at times, it is possible to strengthen your intuition and receive psychic information through more than one psychic 'sense'. Psychic skills are perception abilities that are based on your inner senses, or intuition, and correspond to the five conventional senses: seeing, hearing, feeling, smelling and tasting.

As you discovered earlier, we have more ways of perceiving than through the usual five senses. Moreover, what each sense perceives can impact what another sense perceives. This is referred to as **multisensory** perception, in which all of our senses work together to provide us with a complete picture of what is going on in our environment.

More interestingly, what you can perceive is NOT limited to the information that each sense feeds to your brain;

you can sense with your whole body. When you sit on a plane, for example, what you see changes as the plane lifts off; the cabin in front of you seems higher, but nothing else in your range of vision has changed. Your ear canals are informing you if you are tilting backwards, which changes what you view. Another example would be carrying a cup. When you look at your cup, you see that it is facing you. However, since you touch and feel it, your brain receives extra information and you recognize it as a three-dimensional item. In this case, your visual and touch senses work together to provide you with a complete picture.

Similarly, you may discover that when you begin to develop one psychic skill, another emerges. As you begin to see (**clairvoyance**), hear (**clairaudience**), feel (**clairsentience**), taste (known as **clairgustance,** which is the ability to taste a substance without putting anything in one's mouth), or even smell (**clairalience**) with your inner senses, you may discover that they reflect your outer senses. The word '**clair**' comes from the French language and means 'clear'.

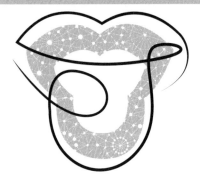

CLAIRGUSTANCE is French for 'clear tasting'. This is the ability to taste something that isn't physically present. This encounter frequently occurs unexpectedly when a deceased loved one attempts to transmit a memory or association you may have with a certain meal or beverage that reminds you of them. A medium, for example would receive messages in this manner. If you have an acute sense of taste, you would be a natural chef, baker or food critic. Identify what flavour you like best in a dish, and get to know the taste of each ingredient, for example. Monitor your progress and discover how you sense this information best. Very often, a person can have more than one dominant conventional sense and this may develop into a having more than one dominant psychic ability.

CLAIRALIENCE means 'clear smelling'. This is the ability to detect odours that have no physical source. Smelling the perfume or cigarette smoke of a deceased relative is an indication of their presence around you and is one example of this. When your sense of smell is strong and clear, you may discover that certain odours evoke memories from your past; you may be drawn to a career as a florist, wine taster or fragrance-maker. Practice getting to know a blend of a scent or a perfume that you like. Notice each smell separately. Get to know what scents you like or make you feel better, for example. If you are so inclined, this may just turn out to be your dominant psychic ability.

The Four Clairs

Developing your psychic ability is like going on a journey. You may begin with a single destination, yet end up having an intriguing adventure on the way. It is really about the journey and how you develop your self-awareness. One thing is certain: your physical body, conventional senses and awareness serve as the basis and building blocks for growing your psychic perception. Here are the four main 'clair' sensing abilities:

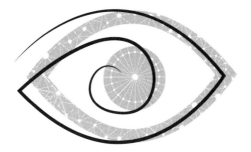

CLAIRVOYANCE (CLEAR SEEING)

Clairvoyance is inner seeing, or the ability to see images. Some use the terms 'clairvoyant' and 'psychic' interchangeably; however, clairvoyance is only one of four 'clair' talents that a psychic has. People with clairvoyant potential are 'visual people' who understand or relate to visual information.

Clairvoyant messages appear as pictures or scenes. Frequently, the image or scene is a metaphor rather than an actual image. If you receive an image of someone wearing a crown, it may indicate that this person will have a prosperous or happy life rather than becoming a king! Your best bet is to create your own dictionary for the images you receive and try to figure out what they represent to you and then how to explain them in the context of the entire message.

In clairvoyant sensing, glimpses of the past, present and future pass in your mind's eye, or third eye, similar to a daydream. You may be naturally a visual person and may be able to grasp an idea better when you see it expressed or written or drawn out as an image on a computer screen or on a canvas. Visual people frequently select careers as artists, builders, photographers, decorators, designers and so on. If this sounds familiar, your clairvoyance is most likely your dominant sense.

As your clairvoyant abilities grow, you may notice one or more of the following signs: seeing sparkling light balls or orbs; floating shadowy figures; or colourful dots floating in the air from the corners of your eyes – mostly when you are comfortable, daydreaming or 'zoned out'. Another evidence of clairvoyant skill is having vivid dreams. Dreams are usually quite lifelike, with vibrant colours and excellent resolution. This is common since clairvoyance is based on visual impressions.

Furthermore, if you are artistically oriented and are moved by visually beautiful objects, such as art, flowers and sculpture, then you are already prone to visual expressions. Everyone isn't. Some people are uninterested in the arts or any other sort of visual expression. So, you may have natural tendency to developing clairvoyant skills. Don't be surprised if you can see auras of people too, or perceive images and colours in their auric field. People with clairvoyant potential can naturally understand shapes and colours too. They have a sense of how physical objects fit, how colour is coordinated, or how a design flows. Often, they are naturally gifted interior decorators and designers. If you are in business, for example, devising flow charts for a project or a business plan comes easily to you. As a hiker or a mountaineer, reading maps seems like a breeze.

Keep in mind, however, that all psychic 'gifts' may have disadvantages. Many untrained psychics and naturally gifted people struggle to cope with their abilities at first. This is not unusual, or anything you should feel ashamed of. Pablo Picasso, for example, despite being one of the most famous artists of all time, battled with dyslexia and had difficulty studying.

Picasso's perspective of reality was influenced by dyslexia, a language-based learning disability with a visual component. This surely had an impact on his work. It is also what inspired him to pursue painting despite being labelled as 'reading blind' and dropping out of school.

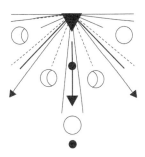

STRENGTHENING YOUR CLAIRVOYANT ABILITIES

Clairvoyance is the ability to see things that aren't visible to the naked eye. It is linked to the sixth chakra, or third eye, because it gives you the ability to 'see clearly' (see Chapter Three on the auric field starting on page 118). This is attributable to the fact that the majority of your visions will be seen through your mind's third eye. The third eye is located immediately above the nose, in the middle of the two brows.

It's critical to concentrate on developing and opening this chakra centre. Furthermore, you must hone your talents in order to have control over them. This will assist you in reducing some of the worry and anxiety that plagues inexperienced psychics. As a result, make a conscious effort to practice employing visual stimulus to train your mind's eye.

Here are a few examples:

FOCUSING ON THE THIRD EYE: Close your eyes and focus on the third eye while regulating your breathing. As you concentrate on the area above your nose and between your brows, allow yourself to be receptive to impressions. Take note of any images or colours that occur in that location after some time has passed. When you're finished, softly wriggle your toes, remember the room you're in, and gently return to present consciousness. You can keep track of your development while you practice by keeping a notebook of your observations.

SENSE YOUR MAIL: Before opening your post or packages you receive in the mail, hold the envelope or package between your palms for a minute or so. Close your eyes and try to sense what is inside. What are the contents of the package? What is the purpose of the letter? Do not be sceptical of the information you are receiving. Allowing your perception to flow will strengthen your third eye over time. To find out what is inside, open the letter or package and check your accuracy. If you continue this for a month or so, you will see an improvement in your accuracy.

SENSING PICTURES: Have a friend or partner cut out a person's image from a magazine, for instance, and place it inside an envelope. For a week, keep this envelope in the same location. Select a time when you will be able to practice clairvoyance by sensing any information about this image. Is the picture of a man or a woman? Young or old? Happy or sad? These are some of the questions you can ask your mind as you tune into the image. To begin with, you can feel the envelope's surface with your fingertips or touch it with your hand.

After that, attempt to check in at the same time every day when you are relaxed by focusing your mind on your third eye and noting what you notice. Check out the photo at the end of the week. If you enjoy this exercise, ask your friend to replace the picture with a new one – and keep practicing! Try to start with simple, clear pictures of people. Then ask your friend to use pictures of objects or locations, for example, as you make progress. This is a simple and potent exercise to train your psychic muscles.

HANDWRITING: Have friends or family members write a paragraph for you, or look at signatures. Begin with a clean slate and an open mind. As you drift into a meditative state, keep gazing at the writing and taking notes on what you see in each piece. Signatures and handwriting are similar to fingerprints. They can reveal a great deal about a person and will get your psychic juices flowing.

In fact, visual stimulation can aid in the development of clairvoyant skills. Visiting art galleries, for instance, is a fun way to do this. As you stand back and gaze at a painting, notice how you are feeling and what impressions you are getting about the work of art or the artist. When you are looking at a portrait, for example, imagine what kind of a person they are, what you can learn about them, as you gaze at their portrait. Often, asking your mind for more information as you are relaxed will help activate your clairvoyant abilities. When you're comfortable, asking your thoughts for more information can help you activate your clairvoyant skills. The more observant you are of what you see with your eyes, the better at clairvoyance you will become.

CLAIRAUDIENCE (CLEAR HEARING)

Clairaudience is inner hearing, or the ability to hear sounds and voices. Mediums often employ this type of skill to communicate with spirits. Clairaudient communication is frequently quiet and serene, with direct and brief messages. Sometimes the message is as simple as one word or number. You may feel as if someone is whispering to you in your head. The voice, on the other hand, is never harsh or cruel. It is frequently calm and stable. It is, if you will, a thought that pierces your mind rather than a thought that your mind projects outwardly.

There will be instances when you hear words, noises, or music in our own mind. More often, it would be in your own voice, just like when you hum a song in your mind. However, Spirit may be able to produce audible sound on rare instances, but this requires a vast amount of focused energy. This form of mediumship is referred to as **trance mediumship**; it happens when you go into a deep trance, and Spirit may 'speak' through your own voice box, or throat.

Trance mediumship needs much disciplined training. In this case, you will have the sense of 'hearing' a spirit's ideas before they are vocalized through you. Messages frequently offer greater direction, for the highest benefit, and are NOT like the voices created by a person suffering from mental illness or having a psychotic episode. The former entails leaving reality behind and entering another level of awareness.

Clairaudience is intuitive guidance to your current degree of awareness. You will be more receptive to guidance when you are in a relaxed state and consciously allow yourself to be 'receptive'. Any trepidation will trigger your doubts and bring your brain state to an alert state, taking you out of a meditative state, and your guidance will be incoherent – if it happens at all.

More importantly, self-development is necessary for the development of any psychic abilities, particularly clairaudience. As a person, the more developed and aware you are, the more meaningful and coherent messages you will be able to 'channel'. To attune to Spirit and connect to higher sources of guidance, you must have a higher vibration. It's not about learning a technique to raise your vibration. It is a state of being that arises from your way of life, including your awareness, thoughts, emotions and actions.

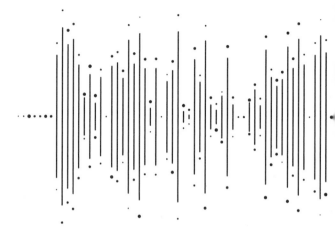

As you develop your intuitive skills, you will be
able to recognize the difference between your inner
guidance, or gut feeling, and clairaudient messages.
Clairaudience is the voice of your higher awareness, or
Spirit you receive telepathically in your own voice. It
is frequently kind, truthful and genuine guidance for
your highest good. Receiving messages from friends,
relatives or acquaintances who passed away is known as
mediumship. Often, they would sound as they did while
they were alive.

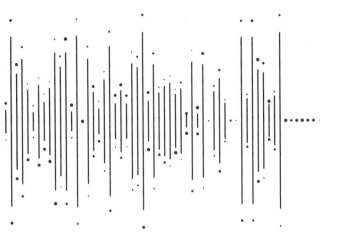

If you retain and absorb information better when it is conveyed aloud, expressed as a spoken word, or music, for example, rather than visually and by being written down, you may have auditory talents. Such individuals frequently become accomplished musicians, singers, writers and public speakers. If this appears acceptable, clairaudience might be a useful sense for you.

Unintelligible sounds, names or phrases, specific words or music may be heard. When your clairaudient skills begin to develop, you may feel ringing or pressure changes in your ears, such as popping or buzzing noises, or you may begin to hear voices. If you are clairaudient, you most likely also have the capability of 'clear speaking'. This indicates your ability to channel, share and speak the messages you 'hear' from spirits as a channeller, medium or trance-channel. These sounds may be different from the ones we are used to hearing. It might sound like it's being said directly next to you, within your mind, or reverberating from another realm.

Other indications that you have this ability are if you prefer to learn through listening to podcasts, for example, or if you have a habit of talking to yourself. Most likely you have conversations with yourself in your head or out loud. This originates from a different source than the 'inner critic' or the same old scenarios of doubt or fantasies that play over and over. This is the voice of intuitive guidance!

Furthermore, if listening to music moves you, you may be clairaudient. It is possible that you will like creating music as well. Many songwriters have heard or dreamed of a tune playing within their heads before putting it down on paper. Beethoven, one of the world's most famous music composers and pianists of classical music, created a wholly unique musical style that reflected his sorrows as he began to go deaf. Beethoven created his finest works in 1820, when he was nearly completely deaf – including the famous Ninth Symphony. If you start seeing images in your mind's eye that correspond to the words of a song, it might indicate that you are clairvoyant too, and can see and perceive energy.

One sure indicator that you have clairaudient abilities is if you prefer to be left alone to enjoy quiet time on your own. Though many people mistake a need for quiet time for an introvert trait, it is also a sign of a sensitive soul that requires time alone to hear its own wisdom. Generally, clairaudients are extremely sensitive, both emotionally and physically, which explains why noises might make you feel tired and irritable.

STRENGTHENING YOUR
CLAIRAUDIENT ABILITIES

You are endowed with clairaudient abilities at birth.
You can start to experience it with practice. Your
clairaudient abilities will grow by putting in a lot
of practice time. Clairaudience is linked to the fifth
chakra, commonly known as the throat chakra. This
chakra governs verbal communication and hearing.
Consider clairaudience similar to tuning a musical
instrument. You may train your hearing to recognize
minor differences in tones by becoming aware of
what to listen for. Here are some practices to help you
improve your clairaudience:

LISTENING: The most straightforward technique to improve your clairaudience abilities is to practice sensitizing your conventional hearing. Close your eyes and sit in a quiet room (or a garden). Tune in to the sounds around you. Gently, you will become conscious of sounds that you were previously unaware of. In a room, for example, you might start to hear distant traffic, an air conditioner buzzing, leaves rustling outdoors, people conversing in another room, or even your own breathing. A variety of birds singing, etc., can be heard in a garden. See if you can isolate and focus on each sound for a few moments. This may be difficult at first, but as you practice, your range of hearing will increase and you will be able to pick up noises from the Spirit realm more easily.

BLOCKING YOUR EARS is another technique to try. Relax by putting earplugs in your ears and lying down in a quiet room. Concentrate on your breathing until you discover your natural rhythm, then shift your focus to your inner world, your body's sounds. The symphony of sound that occurs within the body will astound you. You'll be more conscious of your heart pumping, blood swooshing about your head, and other bodily functions. This approach may appear intimidating at first, but with practice, you will be able to distinguish subtle sounds and improve your clairaudient skills.

MEDITATION: Try meditation with music, spoken and silent meditations, and see which method you prefer most. Next, incorporate a meditation period into your daily routine. Nowadays, you can access a variety of guided meditations online. Keep searching until you find the ideal music or voice with which you connect. Moreover, listening to music can sometimes elicit strong emotions in you. Experiment with feeling what information about the piece of music or the singer's voice you can perceive.

If you are already used to meditating, ask questions in your mind about any information you are receiving. Keeping a 'conversation' going with your higher self, or guides, improves clairaudient communication and gives you more information. Be specific. Ask to receive clairaudient guidance about an issue you are struggling with, for instance. Concentrate on this single question and seek guidance. Messages from the Higher Spirits can be heard during a conversation, through the words of a song on the radio, or through a random sound. So next time you turn the radio on, notice what songs come up!

CLAIRSENTIENCE (CLEAR FEELING)

Clairsentience is inner sensing or recognizing feelings and emotions. It is perhaps the most practical of all intuitive abilities. If you like, it is the ability to interpret the feelings of others. For example, sensing the collective energy of a room, an individual or an object you touch is an example of clairsentience (the latter is known as psychometry; see chapter 5).

Clairsentients are also able to retrieve information from dwellings, public buildings and outdoor locations without physically being there. As such, it is normally associated with the sixth sense. This requires sensing the energy field of a person (including their emotions, and even physical pain), or a location. It all boils down to being aware of changes in one's own energy field (see Chapter Three). Clairsentients, in essence, are aware of a stream of energetic vibrations flowing through their own bodies and emotions.

You might already be clairsentient without even realizing it. For example, you may have a strong 'gut' sensation, whether positive or bad, about someone you just met or a place as you enter it. Sometimes you may get the 'chills' for no apparent reason. You may be tuning into the emotional energy or information contained inside the energy field of a person, a spirit or a location.

Remember that clairsentient messages manifest as feelings. You may experience those feelings physically in your body, as though you are going through those emotions yourself. Clairsentience is also associated with the sense of touch (hot, cold, smooth, coarse, pleasing or displeasure as examples). Become aware of how you feel when you touch different textures, people or objects.

You may sense that someone is excited, joyful, serious, outgoing or smart, for example. You may also be picking up on an event they are about to go through, such as getting married, or one they have recently gone through, like an ailment such as indigestion, when you sense a tingling in your gut.

When a message is important for the person you're sensing, you may feel a cold all over your body. To discover more about how you receive psychic information and how your body reacts, simply keep a notebook and document your experiences. As a result, your intuition will be sharper and you will understand how to interpret what your body is sensing.

Clairsentients can also sense what went on in a room, for example, as soon as they walk into it. If a strong debate or disagreement took place, they are able to sense it even without witnessing it or being informed of what took place. That is why crowded places or spending extended periods of time with a large number of people can be exhausting for them.

If you naturally have a more dominant clairsentient ability, you will be able to tell what kind of person someone is just by looking at him or her when you first meet.

Sometimes you find yourself steering a friend away from a certain individual who later turns out to be toxic, or a complete fraud, but you cannot explain how your instincts helped make that critical decision. Moreover, you might also feel strongly connected to a place or the energy of a particular location, such as a sacred place. You will find yourself visiting often, or thinking about it when you are there. This is because you resonate with the energy of that space, or its energy field (see Figure 4 in Chapter Three).

Clairsentients are highly sensitive to their surroundings. In fact, if you were to see a dramatic film in which the characters undergo tragic events, you might feel powerful emotions. It is a good idea to surround yourself with a shield of light all around you. You can do this just by thinking of it, or imagining it. This decreases any unfavourable impacts on you.

When you develop self-awareness, you will become highly sensitive and in tune with not just your own feelings, but also the feelings of others. In other words, you will be able to empathize. This is what makes humans natural healers and caregivers. People who easily sympathize with others are generally driven to seek occupations as doctors, therapists, counsellors, nannies, instructors or horticulturists. If this describes you, clairsentience is at the top of your list of abilities. And, by the way, if you are frequently told that 'you are too sensitive,' you are most likely an empath – a solid marker of high clairsentient potential.

STRENGTHENING YOUR CLAIRSENTIENT ABILITIES

Clairsentience is associated with the fourth chakra: the heart. This is not surprising since the heart has its own nervous system. The heart picks up information immediately and feeds it to the brain. For example, when you walk into a property, you will feel instantly either relaxed or that you want to walk out! What is often referred to as 'gut feeling' is actually 'heart feeling'. Your first impressions are usually right! This chakra connects thoughts, emotions and spirituality, and is linked to our ability to empathize, the depth to which we can care for others, emotional openness, self-awareness, self-reflection, and how tranquil we feel within ourselves. Learning how to open the Heart Chakra is a beautiful experience, and it will allow you to build your psychic abilities on a healthy foundation.

Dr. Ali M Alshami, Department of Physical Therapy, College of Applied Medical Sciences, Imam Abdulrahman Bin Faisal University, Saudi Arabia, wrote about Dr. Armour's discovery in 1991, in his medical paper published in the National Library of Medicine in 2019, that the heart has a neural network made up of approximately 40,000 neurons that are similar to neurons of the brain. "The heart sends more signals to the brain than vice versa." He went on to say that "important changes occur in brain regions that are influenced by cognitive and emotional aspects" – what you think and feel.

You already have this built-in gift. And now you have the opportunity to transform clairsentience into the true gift that it is. Simply being able to feel and understand another person's pain can increase love and compassion in a relationship, whether you are a friend, counsellor, shopkeeper or gardener. Of course, if you are a therapist or a healer, this ability is invaluable. Clairsentience can help you build a better picture of your client and understand their issues and where they stem from.

Here are some activities to help with the development of your clairsentient abilities:

YOUR ENVIRONMENT: People who are clairsentient are extremely sensitive to their surroundings. Clutter can impair your ability to think and perform in general. So, before you start developing your clairsentient abilities, pay attention to your surroundings. If order, harmony and aesthetics are important to you, start decluttering on a regular basis. Clutter and a chaotic environment can obstruct your ability to perceive. So intentionally invite more positivity into your life and transform your living space into a place where you feel relaxed and at ease. Updating your living area allows you to clear out old, negative energy and welcome in fresh, positive energy. You will now have a wonderful open room to meditate in and do psychic development exercises to improve your clairsentience.

OBJECT SENSING: Practicing **psychometry** is another approach to enhance your clairsentient abilities. This means psychically 'measuring' or assessing the energy of an object. Hold objects between your palms and tune in to how you feel as you hold it. The object can be a

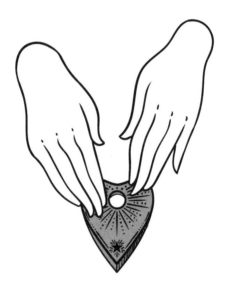

crystal that you want to buy, for example, or an antique-store item that you like. Close your eyes and run your fingertips along the object for a few moments. Try to sense what kind of energy it gives, as well as the energy of its owner.

As you hold the object, notice how you feel. You may receive inaccurate answers at first, but with practice, you will see a significant improvement. As you progress, try an object that belongs to someone you know and is worn by the owner, such as a watch, a necklace or a ring. The more a person wears an item, the more energy or information it contains. If you start receiving images or thoughts about the object, ask your mind 'what does that mean?' and more information will flow. When you are finished, ask your friend for feedback. How accurate were you? Did your reading make sense to them? Keep track of your improvement as you practice, and you will be surprised at how simple and accurate your clear sensing becomes.

PHOTOGRAPHS: One of the most enjoyable exercises to improve your clairsentience is to read another person by tuning in to picture. This is similar to the previous practice of sensing picture to improve clairvoyant abilities, but you will take it a step farther. Request that a friend or family member show you a photograph of someone you've never met but whom they know well. Examine the photograph and try to focus on the person's eyes and tune in to their energy at the time the photograph was taken.

The simplest way is to ask yourself questions about this person in your head. It's a good idea to start with logical observations and then let your imagination run. In your mind, consider if this person was joyful or worried at the time the photograph was shot. Do you get feelings of rage and stress? What kind of person are they? Can they be trusted? If this is your first time practicing clairsentience, you may only be able to detect fundamental negative or good vibrations. Once you're done, request feedback from your friend. How accurate were you? This exercise can be done as many times as you wish to improve your skills further.

REFLECTING ON PAST RELATIONSHIPS: This is an excellent technique for increasing your self-awareness and triggering your clairsentient skills. Make a list of people who have had a positive or negative impact on your life. Put them in chronological order based on when you first met them. Then draw a timeline with their names, the year you met them, and how old you were at the time. Take a look at your timeline. Was there anything else noteworthy going on in your life at those times? Write a one-sentence description of it.

Re-examine your timeline and begin concentrating on the first name. Recall the first memory you have of them, possibly the first time you met. What do you feel when you visit that place in your thoughts and replay that memory now? Write a paragraph beneath that name detailing your first impressions of them, and what you're feeling about them now that you are revisiting the scene. Repeat for each name, allowing time for your mind to process the information. Take a break when you are done, make yourself a cup of tea or coffee, and then sit down and read what you wrote. You will be surprised at what you have already sensed about them and yourself, although subconsciously.

CLAIRCOGNIZANCE (CLEAR KNOWING)

Claircognizance refers to inner knowing. This is the ability of a person to acquire knowledge without knowing how or why they did so. For example, you may come up with an answer to a question without thinking about it. Or you may know individuals, their names, or even events without previously having any knowledge of them. Information just pops out of nowhere into your mind.

Another example: if you have this psychic ability, you will quickly recognize when someone is dishonest or is not to be trusted, or you will just know that you must apply for that job. It is simply knowing things without any solid support.

PREMONITIONS

A premonition is sometimes just a forewarning of something that will happen in the future. A thought just pops into your head out of nowhere. Do you recall a time when you walked out of your door, only to walk back in soon afterwards because you had a 'gut feeling' that you had left the back door open, or even the oven on, only to find out that you were right? It is simply that sense of knowing that something is real, or will be, although you have no logical explanation to back this.

You might think that Claircognizance requires a great deal of faith because you cannot logically explain to yourself why you suddenly 'know' something that you did not know before. However, more research is being performed about this, and scientists have already coined this ability as 'pre-feeling' – which you read about in Chapter Two. There's a lot more that is built into your body, nervous system and brain than you realize!

One way to find out if you are claircognizant is if you often find yourself interrupting people in the middle of their conversation. If so, you do not do so because of bad manners, but because you know what the person with whom you are conversing is going to say. This is also a sign of Claircognizance. You interrupt and sometimes answer before the other person has finished their sentence, because you anticipate what is about to happen or what they are about to say.

Furthermore, Claircognizants just know when not to accept or reject an invitation, for example, or when an offer is too good to be true, or when a person can be trusted without having a logical explanation for what they sense. If that has ever happened to you, then it is a sign that you have a strong claircognizant ability. Have you ever been jolted awake from a deep sleep with a solution to a problem? This suggests that your 'gut feeling' is working even when you are not awake.

STRENGTHENING YOUR CLAIRCOGNIZANT ABILITIES

RESTFUL SLEEP: When it comes to developing any of your psychic powers, especially claircognizant abilities, the first step is to ensure that you get enough sleep! It will help you not only recharge and feel refreshed, but also process what you see and feel as you practice growing your psychic abilities. Your brain continues to function even when you are sleeping. In fact, it does a lot of work in your sleep. It helps to keep you safe, for example, sustaining your breathing and maintaining other biological processes within your body.

What is really interesting is other brain activities that take place in your sleep. Your brain resets itself, filters out neurocircuits, or beliefs that are no longer useful for you, and constantly and effortlessly organizes and conceptualizes everything you experience. This is how the brain helps us bring meaning to our experiences. Much more happens while you are sleeping (see the section on brain networks and dreams). For the time being, consider a restful sleep to be the foundation for safely – and naturally – growing your psychic abilities. Your brain is already equipped to assist you in developing psychic abilities.

USE AFFIRMATIONS: Cognizance is a state of knowledge that entails self-awareness. Positive affirmations are a self-help technique that converts statements about your goals into actions. Saying, or writing, daily affirmations, out loud or in your head, can help you overcome self-doubt, self-sabotage and fear. The best time to practice your affirmations is right before going to bed. Affirmations trigger neural pathways and change the parts of your brain that make you joyful and optimistic. Consider it a means of deliberately transforming your negative thoughts, concerns and doubts into positive thoughts regarding the areas in which you wish to reprogram your brain to support you.

Daily positive affirmations, according to Psychologist Lauren Alexander, PhD, at Cleveland Clinic's Akron General Health & Wellness Green in Ohio, USA, can help you face the world with confidence in yourself and your abilities. When you repeat them often, and believe in them, you can start to make positive changes.

TIPS FOR
Writing a Powerful Affirmation

1 Make a list of the things you want to change.

2 Begin with "I am ...". It is a more effective way of addressing your mind.

3 Write your statement in the present tense.

4 State your new belief briefly. A short message directing your brain is more effective than a long one.

5 Maintain a positive attitude daily in what you say, feel and do.

6 Incorporate feeling into the affirmation.

The final step is critical for affirmations to be effective. The more you engage your physical body in experiencing the outcome of your affirmation, the more it registers in your mind and appears credible to your brain. Feel the relief of accomplishing your objectives in every cell of your body. Feeling the physical manifestation of your new aims assists you to exceed your own emotional boundary. You are more inclined to accomplish something if you 'feel' like you have done it.

From experience, the most effective way is to say your affirmations while you are focusing on your eyes in a mirror. You might feel silly to begin with. However, as you relax and get used to it, the message gets through to your subconscious mind. You are 'consciously' reprogramming your subconscious.

However, using positive affirmations does not mean persuading yourself to deny the difficulties in your life. 'Standing in front of the mirror and saying, "You're amazing" and "You're lovely" can feel extremely inauthentic,' adds Dr. Alexander. Instead, choose positive affirmations that acknowledge the reality of your current belief or situation, while invoking your own ability to press on and grow. Dr. Alexander says. 'I advocate for affirmations that acknowledge the difficulty you're going through but also remind you of times when you've been successful.'

Here are a few suggestions for affirmations to develop your psychic powers that you may find helpful:

"*I am open and ready to receive guidance from the highest source.*"

"*I am open and ready to receive guidance for my highest good.*"

"*I am always guided to the best path for me.*"

"*I am growing my psychic skills gently and safely.*"

"*I am always protected and safe.*"

"*I am equipped with all that I need to grow my psychic skills and be guided.*"

"*Guidance always comes to me at the right time.*"

Check in with Your Body

Your intuition communicates with you through your body, and the more you practice somatic awareness, the more attuned you will become. Somatic awareness is when you recognize your own self within your surroundings. That is, registering any sensations you experience within a situation and identifying their effect on you psychologically, physiologically and socially. For example, do you feel calm or anxious in a particular situation?

Notice if you get an uneasy physical sensation while deciding on an issue, opportunity or meeting with people. Do you have an open, lighter feeling or do you feel heavy? Do you get a tight feeling in your tummy or a sudden headache? It could be stress responses caused by misguided concern, but it could also be your intuition speaking loudly and plainly. Somatic awareness assists you in identifying helpful recommendations, individuals or environments. Your body has already developed to detect sensations and send messages to your brain to determine the best outcome for you. All you have to do is be present and conscious of what you are experiencing.

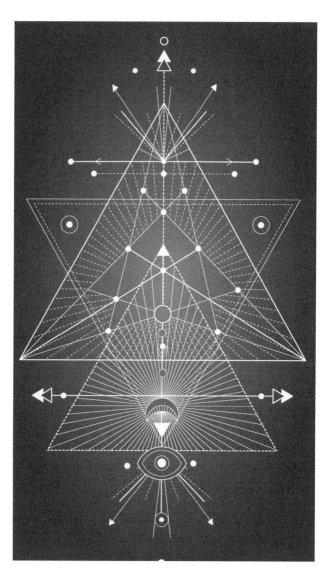

CHAPTER THREE

THE
AURIC FIELD

'*The aura given out by a person
or object is as much a part of
them as their flesh.*'

LUCIAN FREUD, BRITISH PAINTER

To put it simply, you are already equipped to perceive information psychically. This is because your brain perceives all data as electrical pulses through the energy field that exists all around us. All living beings and objects have an energy field.

Psychic Perception through Energy Fields

Figure 4 opposite depicts the interconnection of two energy fields in a straightforward manner. It may be useful to keep this in mind when practicing psychic communication or perceiving information 'instantly' once in an altered state. The two energy fields carry data or information, and when they link, an exchange of information occurs between the two fields (see the following section on the interconnected universe).

In living beings, this energy field surrounds and penetrates the physical body, and is referred to as **The Human Energy Field** or **aura**. We are able to perceive information psychically through the aura, which carries

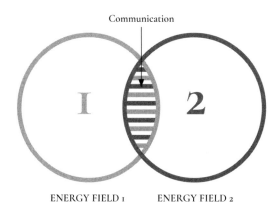

FIGURE 4 Communication between energy fields

a lot of information including the memory of biological functions, a personal emotional and mental wellbeing.

If energy field 1 represents your aura field, energy field 2 can represent a person, an object, a place or location, or an animal!

It follows that the aura is closely connected with our physical health, as well as the wellness of each area and organ in our body. Ancient people, who were closely connected to nature, knew this. In several ancient traditions, like Chinese and Indian, this energy field, Prana, or Chi was recognized and formed the basis of traditional Ayurvedic medicine, and **Traditional Chinese Medicine** (TCM), respectively. They were aware that the body is connected to an energy field, and interacts with it.

High Sense Perception

When you perceive information from an energy field, communication happens between your energy field and the person, object or place that you are perceiving. This process is referred to as High Sense Perception (HSP) or Extra Sensory Perception (ESP). The energy field can be perceived through your inner senses when your brain is in the lower-frequency waves.

"HSP is a way of perceiving things beyond the normal range of human senses," as Barbara Ann Brennan explains in her book *Hands of Light: A Guide to Healing through the Human Energy Field*. Brennan was a research scientist for NASA, following her M.S. in atmospheric psychics, and was one of the pioneers of understanding and healing the human energy field. Perceiving information from the auric field happens when you are in an 'altered state'.

So when your brain is not busy focusing on problem-solving, it still perceives and processes 'subtle' information when you are relaxed. In what is referred to as an **altered state**, you perceive this information as a psychic experience or intuition. Developing **higher intuition** comes with training your brain. What makes it possible to tune in to other energy fields is our own energy field, or **aura** (a system of energy fields composed of seven main **chakras**).

Energy exists everywhere, and 'communications' or interactions between energy fields is ever present (see Figure 4). In the human energy field, or aura, a chakra is an energy portal, or wheel, where the pathways of the human energy field are focused. Our auras, which derive from the Greek word for 'breeze', reflect our moods, feelings and general vibe. Essentially, our auras give off our first impressions before we can even say hello. There are often several colours in any one aura. Each colour is thought to represent a distinct layer of our energy field. The way these colours change and interact reflects the emotional, spiritual and physical complexities of a person and what went on in their life.

Interconnected Universe

The idea that everything in our universe is interconnected is not new. In 1964, J.S. Bell, a physicist, published Bell's theorem, supporting the idea that subatomic 'particles' are connected in some way that transcends space and time. As such, anything that happens to one particle affects other particles. Moreover, this impact is instantaneous and does not

require 'time' to be transmitted. In Bell's theorem, which is now being supported by experimentation, effects can be '**superluminal**', or faster than the speed of light.

Another renowned scientist, Dr. David Bohm, an American-British scientist who has been described as one of the most significant theoretical physicists of the 20th century, stated the same thing about quantum physics – "There would be non-local connections of distant particles" – meaning that, although objects may be very far from each other, there is still a subtle connection between them.

So, in an altered state, you are able is communicate with this energy field. Through training and practice, it will be possible for you, too, to perceive information (instantly) from other energy fields (see Figure 4).

Interpreting Information

How you interpret this information depends on
what your brain knows, and how conscious you
are of experiences you have had. The level of your
personal awareness, understanding all the 'data' of
your experiences (how you interact with life), seems to
be an important factor in how your brain interprets
information. So remember to keep a journal of your
psychic journey. At the very least, it will help you build
your own dictionary of interpretation. At the very best,
it will assist and enrich your personal growth as you
develop your psychic abilities.

Multi-Dimensional Reality

In your everyday life, as you go about your tasks, you are conscious and focused. Your brain helps you make sense of your environment through the main physical senses. Your brain also perceives time in a linear manner: yesterday, today and tomorrow. This perception is necessary to help you cope with daily life. However, in altered states, perception of time and physical reality differs.

Another physicist, Jack Sarfatti, suggests that in psychoenergetic systems – the interaction of consciousness, energy and matter – the way superluminal connectedness can exist is through a higher plane of reality.

The Human Aura

The aura is the means through which healing, psychic perception, astral travel, mediumship, remote viewing, etc. is possible. Ancient cultures not only recognized energy, but also saw how it flows along meridian lines that connect the physical body to the aura, how energy flows around the body. In TCM, each organ has its own energy, vibration, sound, specific memory or emotion and is related to one of the five elements in nature (see Table 2). Energetic imbalances in the aura can be corrected through healing, for example, which then filters down to the physical body.

However, there are other factors involved in healing distorted energy patterns. For instance, if the distorted pattern has been established for a long time, it may take few sessions to correct that pattern, while recent patterns respond to balancing more quickly. Similarly, if a distorted pattern persists in the human energy field, without being balanced, it may affect the physical organ itself where the imbalance occurs. Both fields are interconnected and interact with each other.

TABLE 2: TCM FIVE ELEMENT THEORY

ORGAN	ASSOCIATED ORGAN	SOUND
Lungs	large intestine	sssssss
Kidneys	bladder	choooo
Liver	gall bladder	shhhhh
Heart	small intestine	hawww
Spleen	stomach/pancreas	whooo

POSITIVE EMOTION	NEGATIVE EMOTION	ELEMENT	SEASON
courage	sadness	metal	autumn
wisdom	fear	water	winter
generosity	anger	wood	spring
joy	impatience/ insincerity	fire	summer
fairness/ balance	worry	earth	Indian summer

Auras Are Energy Fields

A human aura is made up of seven major layers that vibrate outward from your physical body, one on top of the other. Each layer is linked to the next by an energy hub or wheel known as a chakra, from the ancient Sanskrit language. Together, they make up your aura, or energy field. Understanding the chakra energy system allows you to tune in to and see aura fields, as well as recognize how important your personal growth is in unlocking your psychic potential.

Table 2 shows what type of information each layer of the aura reflects, as well as what you can perceive as you tune in to the colours of any aura, including your own. If you are feeling out of balance, whether physically, emotionally or mentally, it is a good idea not to attempt any psychic-development exercises until you have cleared, recharged and balanced yourself (see examples below).

A chakra is the central hub through which all energy flows in and out of an energy level, and connects it to the next layer. Consider chakras to be energy vortices that spin within us, displaying our level of consciousness as well as our body's wellbeing as they expand outward and interact with other energy fields. They serve as centres of activity for receiving, absorbing and sending data (or energy).

As a result of this combination, chakra vortices arise from the spinal column's central nerve ganglia. Chakra locations also correspond to endocrine glands and a variety of bodily functions such as breathing, digestion and reproduction. In other words, whatever happens inside your body is reflected on the outside in your aura. Similarly, whatever you go through in life on the outside has an impact on your wellbeing on the inside. This explains why, for example, when you are stressed, going for a walk in nature relieves your anxieties, and refreshes and energizes you. As your aura interacts with other energy fields in nature, your field is adjusting and cleansing itself.

The two-way 'communication' between the inside world and the outside environment is ongoing, and is reflected by the changes of aura colours, or vibration. The human energy field is perceived to have seven layers of energy fields, and each layer has a main centre, or chakra. The direct connection between the gland system, the physical body and our energy field offers chakras a psychological interpretation, as shown on the table opposite:

Chakras 2 to 7 have two locations – one in the front of the body, and another at the back of the body.

TABLE 3: PSYCHOLOGICAL FUNCTION OF CHAKRAS

CHAKRA	PSYCHOLOGICAL FUNCTION	COLOUR
Chakra 1	survival	red
Chakra 2	sex	orange
Chakra 3	power	yellow
Chakra 4	love	green
Chakra 5	communication	blue
Chakra 6	imagination	indigo
Chakra 7	spirituality	violet

Chakra 1 vibrates the colour red, is located at the base of the spine, and is connected to the adrenal glands, kidneys and sex organs. Their functions are linked to the formation of internal organs, bones, muscles, blood and bladder. If the energy is low in this chakra, it can manifest as low vitality and general weakness, especially weak legs, for example.

Chakra 2 is distinguished by its orange colour. It is located in the pubic area in the front, and is associated with the reproductive system and the small and large intestines. The back location is the kidney area. A quality of this chakra is vital life energy.

Chakra 3 is yellow in colour and is located in the solar plexus, at the front of the body and in the adrenals in the back. When this centre is obstructed or weak, it affects the digestive organs. For example, a person may experience doubt, fears, anxiety and low self-esteem.

Chakra 4, the Heart Centre, balances our physical aspect with the spiritual, vibrates a green colour, and is located at the heart, front and back.

Chakra 5 is located at the front and back of the throat. It is associated with psychic communication, hearing, speaking, smelling and tasting.

Chakra 6 is located at the front and back of the pituitary gland. Referred to as the third eye, it controls the other major chakras.

Chakra 7, the final main chakra, is referred to as The Crown. It is located just above the top of the head and is associated with spiritual connection, growth, and channelling and receiving inspiration.

There is a two-way communication flow in all energy fields. The flow of energy in a human aura travels up the spine from the initial 'dense' energy layer of the first chakra to the lighter spiritual energy layer of the seventh chakra. This is known as the 'liberating channel' because it is where we let go of negative energy. The 'manifesting channel' runs down the front of the body, from the crown of the head to the bottom of the feet. As you gain knowledge from your experiences, you effectively liberate any trapped or blocked energy in your chakra system, allowing your energy to move up and nourish the next chakra, and so on.

When the liberation channel is clear, your energy field is open to receiving spiritual or intuitive insights that travel down the manifestation channel and into physical reality. For example, an insight or idea enters your mind, and you begin to dream about it, then imagine it, and perhaps later you will talk about it with other people as you become enthralled by it, and so on down the manifestation channel until you materialize it.

Your aura is a living energy field that interacts with your surroundings as well as your life events. If you have a lot of anxiety, for example, and don't deal with it, it will impair your mental wellbeing and how you interpret psychic information. Furthermore, if you have bodily aches and pains, you are less likely to have enough energy to open the upper chakras.

Developing your psychic skills necessitates a holistic approach to your whole wellbeing. Your aura, as a channel for intuition, is closely tied to your own self-awareness. It reflects your personal development as well as your physical, emotional and mental wellbeing. A balanced way of life facilitates the development of psychic abilities since, as a conduit for inspiration and intuition, all aspects of being human must be in balance and function in a healthy manner.

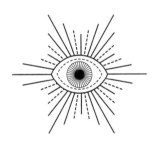

Sensing Chakras

As the energy rises up from the dense, physical first chakra to the spiritual, lighter seventh chakra, the vibration of each chakra changes. This is what determines the colour perception of each chakra centre (as well as the presence of any blockages or unresolved patterns in each). Tuning in to the colours that correspond to each chakra is one approach to perceive the information of each colour, especially if you are interested in healing and understanding how energy works.

Begin by detecting the colour red, then go on to purple, and so on. You can use a colour card deck that authentically depicts the colour of each energy centre. Alternatively, you can create your own colour-card set by using Pantone colours that correspond to each chakra. Another option is to look for films used to change the colour of stage lights, for example.

Start with one colour at a time. Allow yourself enough time, make sure you are not distracted, and begin your adventure by considering each colour fully before moving to the next one. Sense each colour card or film by running the palm of your hand over it, or touching it. You can also stick a colour card on a wall, or hold it between your hands, and meditate on it.

Be conscious of any physical sensations in your body. You may also start receiving mental or visual impressions, for example. Make a note of your exploration for each colour, and note down any thoughts that come into your head as you write.

You may also improvise your own chakra colour visualization. For instance, as you lie down to relax, take a few deep breaths and envision yourself swimming in a clear pool of red-coloured water. How do you feel as you swim in the red water, with all of your senses? Then imagine or pretend that the water changes colour, to orange, then yellow, and so on as you continue to swim along in that imaginary pool.

Be aware of any changes you experience while swimming in each colour. Try to describe the colour's quality: is it heavy or light, invigorating or soothing? Is it hot, warm or cool? Which part of your body is affected by each colour's sensation? What emotions does it evoke in you? Asking such questions in your mind will assist you in determining the quality and type of information communicated by each colour. This is more than simply a mental exercise in tuning in to energy fields; it will sharpen your perception as you explore deeper into the 'bandwidth' of information that colour contains. Swimming in colour visualization also helps to cleanse each of your chakras, restore your aura balance and aid relaxation and restful sleep.

DEVELOPING YOUR INTUITION

'*At times you have to leave the city of your comfort and go into the wilderness of your intuition. What you'll discover will be wonderful. What you'll discover is yourself.*'

ALAN ALDA, AMERICAN ACTOR AND DIRECTOR

opefully you have realized by now that developing clear intuition requires self-awareness and discipline. Psychically perceiving subtle information requires awareness of what you are experiencing through your conventional senses. Identifying how you think, and processing what you go through in life on a daily basis, is also important. If you become emotionally stuck on an experience, for example, you will stifle your psychic development. As you started learning in Chapter Three, information is received through your entire body since intuition is communication between two energy fields.

The vibration of your energy field (or aura), which is made up of the seven major centres, or chakras, influences the quality of your communication with other energy fields. All chakras are linked to one another and interact with one another. As a result, individuals with clear chakras are more balanced and self-aware. And this enables you to become a clear channel for guidance.

Furthermore, the quality of your intuition is reflected in your ability to interpret and learn from the information and guidance you receive. Keeping a psychic journey journal expands your understanding and makes you a wiser and more aware person. Holding yourself accountable for your own psychic development is a great catalyst.

Self-awareness includes:

- Your way of thinking. Your thinking is influenced by how much attention you pay to your life, and how much you learn from your past (really, as it happens). How you feel affects how you think and forms your belief system.

- Current beliefs you hold. A negative mindset limits your development in life. Systematically rewrite your beliefs, using affirmations, for example.

- Knowledge you already have. The more you know, the more you will open up your mind to.

- And holding yourself accountable.

Keeping this in mind allows your psychic abilities to emerge in a more grounded, practical and deliberate manner. It improves your intuition and you start to trust it.

The following section contains practical exercises and tips for improving your intuition. You can, however, start right now by living each day to the fullest. Be present in each moment and focus on information that comes to you through your conventional senses. Take note of what you see, taste, touch, smell and hear. When your mind wanders and you get stuck, ask yourself, 'Where is my mind?' Being self-aware entails focusing and directing your mind.

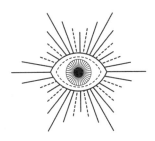

Keep an Open Mind

Your brain does what you tell it to do! It is also crucial to keep an open mind. If you believe you will never be able to develop your intuition, you would be right. Your brain will only do what you tell it to do. Keep an open mind to better understand yourself, and be curious about what you might encounter on your quest of self-discovery. You will be able to tell the difference between information you are receiving psychically and rubbish that your mind is making up.

Also become aware of how your brain receives and processes information. Do you remember a time when you were faced with a difficult issue and suddenly felt, in your gut, that you had the right answer? Intuition is a type of unconscious reasoning that is based on how your brain receives and processes information. So when you go to an interview or meet someone for the first time, pay attention to your actual body and how it reacts to what you see and feel (see the section on Claircognizance starting on page 106).

Pay attention to what you perceive through your conventional senses. Explore each sense mindfully with a variety of images, scents, textures, sounds, etc. and become aware of any patterns you detect, for example, in the behaviour of people you know well, such as friends and family. Patterns are important, as they aid intuition.

The late social scientist Herbert Simon, PhD, explained how your brain naturally organizes these patterns into

chunks of knowledge, a process known as **chunking**. Looking around you, for example, you do not just see shapes and colours. Your brain develops concepts of what you are experiencing and organizes this information into 'chunks'.

That is how you understand that you are looking, for example, at a book, a computer screen, a lamp or a car. Over time, the brain chunks and links more and more patterns together, and stores these information clusters in long-term memory. When you recognize a small detail of a familiar pattern, your brain immediately recognizes the bigger picture, or chunk of information. This neural phenomenon is known as an **intuition-flash**. Being alert, curious, grounded and logical as you live your life will naturally lead you to enhanced perception – and naturally experiencing flashes of intuition.

Brain Networks

Intuitive flashes are sophisticated brain circuitry. They most likely evolved so that our ancestors could swiftly assess a person or situation. This talent was especially important for our female ancestors. They had to tune in to their infants in order for them to survive. This could explain why women have an advantage when it comes to reading people nowadays. So, rather than dismissing your instincts, pay attention to them. Although your intuition is not always correct, especially when you first develop it, it can be a useful first step in decision-making.

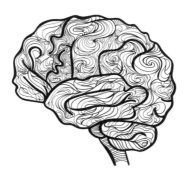

Practicing a creative pastime – anything artistic that you can do on your own – is another activity that generates intuitive flashes. Creativity can significantly improve your psychic perception. Within your brain, there are networks and areas that specialize in a number of tasks. When you are creative, you activate more than one of your major **brain networks**. When you enhance your creative abilities, you engage more than one brain network; these are referred to as **brain-wide** networks.

Brain-wide networks are critical for understanding our thoughts. When you get psychic information, your brain perceives it in a multitude of ways, including ideas, images, sound and so on. Being creative will allow you to develop all of your psychic 'clair' abilities while having fun!

Start a Creative Hobby

Your intuitive abilities emerge from the same side of the brain, the right side, that is mostly responsible for your creative abilities, including your imagination. Clairvoyancy is seeded in imagination. Engaging in creative hobbies is not only relaxing, but also activates your imagination and helps your brain switch between brain networks and brainwaves. It also silences your inner critic, as you are about to find out.

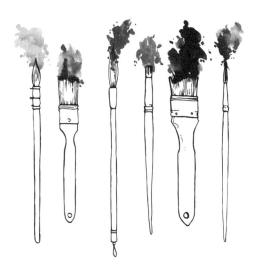

THE NEUROSCIENCE OF CREATIVITY

"When a task requires a thorough level of concentration, the **executive attention network** will be called into play," Tim Newman, senior editor of *Medical News Today*, wrote in 2016. "For example, as you read this, your executive attention network will be busying itself (as long as you are paying attention)." The other brain network, known as **the default network**, constructs images based on your prior experiences and imagines alternate situations and events.

The intriguing part is that when you're daydreaming, your brain isn't focused on the outside world, and "the default network is implicated in functions such as collecting facts about the self, reflecting on personal emotions, and recalling past events."

This network appears to be involved in social cognition and empathy as well; it aids in imagining what another person is thinking (or feeling). This is important for you to understand, since extrasensory abilities are about sensing subtle information with your inner senses through sensations, images, sound, shapes and textures.

The third brain network is known as the **salience network**, and it helps the brain in deciding what to pay attention to. When you think about it, your eyes, ears, tongue, nose and skin are constantly bombarded with sensory stimuli. The salience network helps the brain decide which stimuli to pay attention to and which to ignore. The salience network is thought to be involved in **switching** between relevant neural networks, turning off or on the most appropriate groupings based on its evaluation of a situation.

Driving a car, for example, fills your visual field with road, skies, houses, trees, traffic signals, the steering wheel and a variety of other objects. Despite the wealth of options, the salience network focuses your attention on the woman with the pram who is attempting to cross the road on the right, 500 feet down.

"The ability to switch networks is an important part of creativity." Spending all of your attention, for example, on a creative puzzle may activate the executive attention network. If, on the other hand, your creative endeavour is playing a lovely piece of music on a guitar, "the attention may shift from acute concentration to areas more involved in emotional content and auditory processing." Knowing this about your brain will help you understand how it **connects** with what you experience on a regular basis. The more aware you are of what you are sensing, the more self-aware you will become. What you see, hear, touch, feel and taste can heighten your awareness and inner senses.

Furthermore, the more general information you have, and the more you deliberately notice and become aware of, the more your intuition will develop. For example, if you know what the Grand Canyon looks like and where it is physically, you will have a flash of intuition and know what the image is conveying: a location, for example, where someone is close to or about to visit, and so on. If, on the other hand, you were unfamiliar with the Grand Canyon, even if you psychically perceived an image of it, you would have no idea what it was, or how to begin to understand what you were psychically perceiving!

Creativity may even help you identify which psychic 'clair' you are naturally prone to develop. Do you enjoy photography, sculpture, drawing or some other creative hobby? Start with whichever one appeals to you; it may trigger other creative talents you did not know you had, and trigger your built-in psychic potential.

In fact, learning anything new is beneficial! According to *The National Academic Press* (of Sciences, Engineering and Medicine), "Learning changes the physical structure of the brain." The functional organization of the brain is affected by structural changes. In other words, learning organizes and reorganizes the brain. "Different parts of the brain may be ready to learn at different times." You never know when you will get an intuition flash!

Understand Your Dreams

Your brain is your greatest asset in developing your
intuition. As your brain ticks along in your sleep, it is
sorting out information, helping you solve any problems
you had while awake, or conscious, too. Brain scans have
revealed that we use nearly all of our brain all the time,
even while we are sleeping. So it is worth your time to
pay attention to, and understand, what may appear to
be 'cryptic messages' from your subconscious that come
through as a dream. Understanding your dreams is the
gateway to accessing your psychic abilities in your sleep,
and to connecting your subconscious mind with your
conscious mind. In other words, it will increase your
level of self-awareness.

Dreams account for 30% of your life, and are the
language of your subconscious mind, or what you are
not consciously aware of. Information, life experiences
and beliefs that you hold and are not aware of are 'filed'
or tucked away in your unconscious mind. As your
brain reorganize theses bits of information into relevant
chunks to help you make better decisions in the future,
it does so in your sleep. This neural activity, if you like, is

fertile ground for shaping your dreams during the deep-sleep phase.

As a result, examining your life's experiences by asking questions to your subconscious mind before going to bed can help you discover what is holding you back, for example, to make sense of your experiences. Your awareness of your own life expands, and you grow more conscious, or self-aware. Neurologist Krish Sathian, at Emory University in Atlanta, Georgia, USA, says: "Even when you're engaged in a task and some neurons are engaged in that task, the rest of your brain is occupied doing other things, which is why, for example, the solution to a problem can emerge after you haven't been thinking about it for a while, or after a night's sleep, and that's because your brain's constantly active." Your dreams can, therefore, help you explore the solution or wisdom of any situation, positive or negative, that you may encounter.

Bridging the Unconscious with the Conscious Mind

Understanding your dreams helps you bridge your conscious awareness with your intuition. It is a great way to open up your claircognizant abilities and psychic centres. The fifth and sixth chakras are major psychic centres of psychic communication and clairvoyance, respectively. What is really interesting is the rapid eye movement (REM) that takes place in your deep sleep.

REM is intense brain activity that happens in deep sleep. It creates vivid and active, or lucid dreams. REM sleep rejuvenates your brain and improves memory and learning. Each night, you can have three to five bouts of REM sleep, each lasting around 10 minutes, with the last cycle lasting up to an hour. You experience REM about 90 minutes after falling asleep. As your brain activity increases, your eyes dart around, and your pulse, blood pressure and breathing rate increase.

The movement of the eyes during REM is linked to the pineal gland, at the centre of the brain, whose primary function is producing melatonin, which regulates your sleep patterns, circadian rhythms and reproductive hormones. Moreover, darkness prompts the pineal gland to start producing melatonin while light causes that production to stop. As a result, melatonin helps regulate circadian rhythms and synchronize our sleep-wake cycle with night and day. The pineal gland, located at the base of the skull, parallel to the middle of the eyebrows, is also known as the '**third eye**'.

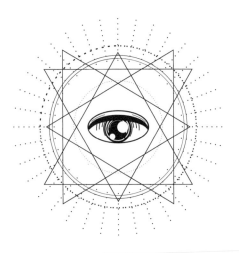

According to Candice Covington, author of *Essential Oils in Spiritual Practice: Working with the Chakras, Divine Archetypes, and the Five Great Elements*, the pineal gland is "the biological relative of the energetic third eye chakra". Its name, the third eye, comes from the pineal gland's primary function, which is sensitivity to light. Or, in other words, 'letting in light and darkness', just as our two eyes do.

During this stage, most people experience lucid dreams – a type of dream where the dreamer becomes aware that they are dreaming. During this stage, too, the right and left hemispheres of the brain are more coherent with each other. **Coherence** allows for information being processed on one side of the brain to be shared with the other side. Both sides, the creative and the logical, are in tandem. This results in increased learning and awareness levels. In other words, you become more conscious of the subtle psychic perception abilities. Wow! Dreaming not only triggers your psychic abilities, but also allows you to make sense of experiences and understand psychic messages that are often delivered in a dream.

You may have even heard the term 'golden brain' used to refer to people who use both sides of their brain equally. Coherence is also what happens as you learn to meditate or practice a creative hobby. In fact, after waking from REM sleep, the mind seems 'hyperassociative' – more receptive to semantic priming effects.

Priming is a cognitive process whereby exposure to one stimulus, or sensory experience, influences a response to a subsequent stimulus, without conscious guidance or intention. "For example, the word NURSE is recognized more quickly following the word DOCTOR than following the word BREAD." People awakened from REM have performed better on tasks like creative problem-solving. Working with your dreams is another fun way to grow your psychic potential and personal awareness.

Dream Language

While there is a universal language to dreams, your own dream language is personal and specific to you. That's why your dreams can offer you valuable insights. The more you work with your dreams, the more you will become aware of how you operate in your life, and what you need to address and work on.

Let's say you have a traumatic memory of a break-up. When this memory is 'stored' in your subconscious for a long while, you begin to unconsciously form negative beliefs and thoughts around having relationships. These beliefs tend to gather together, or chunk, and each thought enforces the other. Effectively, your unconscious mind is building a wall around you, to stop you from having a meaningful relationship, because to your subconscious mind 'relationships are painful'.

So you might dream of lovers abandoning you, or you might even have a nightmare involving a person you have just met. Do not be alarmed if you have a **nightmare**. Nightmares are often a 'cry' from your subconscious mind, asking you to reflect on what you went through and heal your emotions, thoughts and experiences. A nightmare is, therefore, an opportunity to explore, heal, understand and integrate your experiences. You mind creates symbols that represent, or recreate, these situations and experiences in order to attract your attention to 'unfinished business'.

The more you work with your dreams, the more you will become aware of how you operate your life, and the more you will find there is more to know and experience. With perspective, your sense of reality changes, encompassing more of what initially seemed to be outside your immediate field of vision. When your perspective changes, it helps you modify your decisions and actions. So when the next relationship comes around, you'd be fully aware and in command of creating a new desirable outcome.

Start a Dream Journal

Dreams are the bridge between the conscious and subconscious mind. The dream state is also the domain where it is possible to 'experiment' with probable outcomes, or realities, in a safe manner by directing your dreams – that is by asking questions and journalling the answers you receive as a dream. By learning to direct your dreams, you get to know yourself better, and clear yourself as a channel for psychic reception.

Starting a dream journal focuses your mind on a specific issue by giving it a direct question. As your brain 'sees' what is on your mind, you direct your subconscious to release information that is buried deeply, and bring it to your conscious attention. For example, you can write a question asking your subconscious mind, *'Please give me a dream on how to begin trusting my intuition.'* When you wake up, and before you get out of bed or talk to anyone (dreams do evaporate quickly!), write what you remember, no matter how little information there is. You can also write words you woke up with, or describe how you felt – for example, "I woke up thinking about the colour orange" or "I slept very well, woke up feeling good, but do not remember the dream." This is important. Gradually, you will start writing more and more, and recall more of your dreams.

You may use dream direction to explore various alternative outcomes of any situation, before you commit or decide on the matter. For example, you can ask, *"How would I feel about changing jobs, moving house, or marrying X?"* You can safely receive helpful insights into a probable future or outcome before you actually get there. It is similar to 'time travelling' in a meditative state, except this time you ask your subconscious mind to do so while you are asleep!

In your dream journal, maintain the following elements in your entries:

• The date you asked the question.

• A brief description of what is currently going on in your waking life, for example, thinking about moving to a new home.

• The date you had the dream.

• A description of the dream.

• Leave a blank a page to write your notes later on, before you start journalling about a new dream question.

• On the last page of your journal, build a list of personal symbols.

To begin with, especially if you are not used to exploring, or do not usually remember your dreams, write down any sensations, words, colours or feelings you woke up with. With practice, you will begin to remember more of your dreams and eventually notice

patterns in your dreams. Your patterns are **personal dream symbols** that make up your dream language. Personal symbols are themes, people, words, locations or colours that frequently pop up in your dreams.

In a dream, both universal and personal symbols may emerge. Universal symbols have a common significance that people from many cultures and backgrounds see in their dreams. They exist in our collective consciousness, the human-family mind, and are fashioned by our shared aspirations, wants and experiences. Generally, your dreams may represent current events in your life, which your brain is processing. Other times, your dreams will be prompted by conscious or unconscious desires as well as issues you wish to specifically explore (and state as a question in your dream journal). Examples of universal symbols are telephone calls, spiders or rats, houses, schools or colleges, colours, people or locations you do not personally know, and nature's elements, such as water, fire, forests, and wind.

Let's say that you asked about relationships in your journal. You might write down a question, focusing your subconscious mind in the following way: "*Please give me a dream about my future relationship, which I will remember when I wake up.*" Let's say that, in your dream, you saw a spider crawling towards you as you were walking along in the countryside. In the next scene of your dream, you remember swimming in a clear lake that you do not recognize; the water was clear and left you feeling refreshed. In the next scene, you recall receiving a mobile phone call that interrupts your dream, but you wake up feeling happy and refreshed.

Next, list words or elements of the dream that stood out. For example:

• Unknown countryside.

• Swimming in clear water.

• Feeling refreshed.

• Receiving a call on a mobile phone.

• Waking up happy.

Your dream indicates that, while you may be afraid of relationships (the spider is a universal symbol for fear), you may decide to enter a relationship (walking along an unknown path). Swimming in a clear lake represents experiencing a positive emotional tie with someone new (unknown location of both walk and lake). Receiving a mobile-phone call indicates that this message will happen soon (quick or instant communication).

Unknown locations can indicate new experiences in your life, or that events will take place at a future time. Swimming indicates undergoing emotional experiences. When the water is clear, it represents positive emotional ties. If the water is murky or cold, it indicates unfavourable or troublesome emotional ties. Any 'communication' in a dream is about communication – either the need to communicate better or that your dream is delivering your answer. The type of communication can also represent time. Postal letters represent longer time frames. Mobile-phone calls represent that the dream message will happen quickly.

Meditate – It Is Important!

You know by now that developing psychic abilities is about self-growth, how grounded you are and what state your brainwaves are in. Meditation is, therefore, a practical tool to increase your claircognizance or any other psychic skill. It makes no difference whether you wish to increase your claircognizance, clairaudience, clairvoyance or clairsentience; without meditation, your progress will be far slower.

Meditating daily improves brain function, reduces stress, and helps you to connect deeply with your inner-self, people around you, and your inner senses. With practice, you will be able to create a state of calm and tranquillity regardless of what is going on around you. In this way, your psychic development is safe and gentle, and unfolds at a rate appropriate to your growth.

Meditation, or any practice of stillness or quietness such as focusing on your breath, allows you to be calm and also raises your energetic vibration. Because Spirit energy vibrates at a higher frequency, raising your vibration is critical for increasing your psychic talents and being able to receive higher guidance. This is especially true if you are going to practice channelling – what was previously referred to as automatic writing. There are various techniques to meditation. If one doesn't seem to work for you, consider trying a new type before giving up. Also, experiment with listening to guided mediations, or meditations that combine Binaural sounds (see section below).

Listen to Binaural Sounds

Listening to meditations with extra **binaural beats** is one method to get more out of your meditation time. Binaural sounds are frequently used as a background sound in meditations to connect both hemispheres of the brain for optimal benefit of the meditation.

As you already know, brainwaves can range from low frequency to high amplitude and from high frequency to low amplitude. Brainwaves generate binaural beats, which result in diverse mental states that affect your brain in different ways, as mentioned in Chapter One. Binaural beats can also be made in a variety of frequencies to train your brain to achieve a specific mental state. This is referred to as **brain entrainment** because it synchronizes neural activities across the brain. The brain generates an illusion and entrains itself when you listen to binaural beats, which are two tones with slightly different frequencies, at the same time. Please keep in mind that you must listen to binaural beat meditations using a headset or headphones; otherwise, the sounds will have no impact. This is due to the fact that each ear requires a different frequency.

The two tones are interpreted by your brain as a separate beat. The tones interact with your brainwaves to create a beat with a different frequency. This frequency is the difference in Hertz (Hz) between the two tones' frequencies. If you listen to a 440 Hz tone with your left ear and a 444 Hz tone with your right ear, you will hear a 4 Hz tone. When you listen to binaural beats, your brain activity matches the frequency established by the beat's frequency. This is referred to as the **frequency-following** effect.

Binaural beats, added in meditations, enhance the results of the meditation; they can open your heart, for example, or induce relaxation, alleviate stress, or strengthen specific chakras. Binaural beats can also be used to indirectly bring relief from some illnesses. According to scientific research, there is a fine boundary between physical and mental wellness. This indicates that reducing worry and stress in the body will improve physical health. Furthermore, binaural beats cannot be used in place of traditional therapy, but they can be used as a complementary technique, if addressed with a doctor, if you have a mental illness or depression. According to research, binary beats are beneficial to mental health since they promote happy feelings.

Listening to soothing meditations with binaural sound at night may be the best time for you to fall asleep or trigger a dream. Theta beats create theta waves at a frequency of 4 to 8 Hz during stage one of sleep, which is the lightest state of sleep. Daydreaming and free-thinking states are also associated with theta waves. Sleeping can be aided by listening to binaural beats at delta frequencies, for instance.

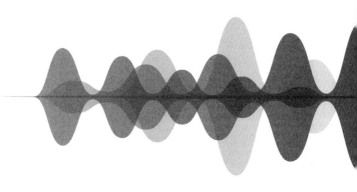

Binaural sounds are thought to be at the cutting edge of sound treatment. Lower beta frequencies (14 to 30 Hz) have been associated with greater concentration and alertness, problem solving and memory. According to a 2020 study, binaural beats of 40 Hz were proven to be beneficial in improving training and learning. Some studies found that listening to particular binaural beats can boost the strength of certain brainwaves. While there are no potential risks to listening to binaural beats, you must ensure that the tone level is not too high. Loud sounds at or over 85 dB can cause hearing loss in the long run.

Numerous binaural beats are freely available on the internet, and people's reactions to the beats differ. Experiment with several to find the ones that work best for you. Binaural beats' effectiveness is determined by the listener. The beats will be effective for certain folks. Others may find them annoying and ineffective. This is where maintaining a journal comes in handy. You can guide yourself if you write down what frequency you listened to and how you felt. This is also a part of strengthening your intuition, because you will be more aware of what benefits your body-mind system.

To begin, we recommend that you listen to binaural
sound meditations calibrated to the frequency of the
heart centre, which is tuned to frequencies that vibrate
with an energy of love and harmony. This corresponds
to a frequency of 221.23 Hz and a binaural frequency of
10.5 Hz. The carrier frequency promotes larger levels
of love energy and the desire for peace, whereas the
beat frequency is related to love of life, love of self and
love of others. This is due to the fact that, as discussed
in Chapter Three about the Human Energy Field,
the heart chakra, or centre, is the gateway to deeper
understanding and unconditional love. It transmutes all
negativity and conflict between higher mind-guidance
and our ego in this lifetime, which is based on our
character, belief system and emotions.

Chant!

Stewart Pearce mentions in his book, *The Alchemy of Voice*, the magical powers of sound vibrations: "Sound is at the core of creation, and the harmonics of certain chants function like keys. Meaning that sacred sound opens portals into transcendental corridors of light, which enable our Spirit Guardians, Angels or highly evolved Ascended Beings to speak with us. I once worked with a Native American Shaman, who illustrated this when he chanted in a darkened Kiva under the Mesa of New Mexico, and the entire chamber lit up with his chant. He suggested later that the pineal gland can be triggered by the magical resonance of certain chanted sounds, whereby phyto-luminescent chemicals are released, bringing forth light that heals!"

The power of your own voice, when you chant, reverberates throughout all of your body, clearing and realigning chakra centres. This is a simple and enjoyable chanting exercise to open, cleanse as well as strengthen your chakras, and develop your psychic skills. Sound vibrates with all the cells in your body, making it a fun and quick method to fine-tune your instrument for psychic communication. Simply take three long breaths, and then exhale to the sound of the chakra on the third. Begin with chakra 1, then chakra 2, and so on.

As you chant, you will become aware of whatever sound is easiest for you to chant. When you can chant all sounds in order, and in one session, it is a sign that your energy field is clear, all of your chakras are balanced, and you are ready to psychically perceive your environment. Your psychic powers are activated by your own breathing and chanting.

TABLE 4: VIBRATIONAL SOUNDS OF CHAKRAS

CHAKRA	PSYCHIC ABILITY	VIBRATIONAL SOUND
Chakra 1	Grounded interpretation	**O** as in **rope**
Chakra 2	Emotional balance	**OO** as in **due**
Chakra 3	Claircognizance, mental awareness	**AH** in **father**
Chakra 4	Clairsentience/ astral travel	**AY** as in **play**
Chakra 5	Clairaudience/ dreams, third eye	**EE** as in **see**
Chakra 6	Clairvoyance	**MMM NNN**
Chakra 7	Channelling	**NGNGNG** as in **sing**

Practice Automatic Writing

What was previously referred to as automatic writing is now referred to as channelled writing or channelling. The term 'automatic' implied something that happens without your knowledge, which was ambiguous, if not misleading.

Channelling is when you allow guidance to come through, rather than 'imposing' your own thoughts, as you would do when you usually write. Channelling trains your mind to open and be ready to receive guidance from your intuition, inner wisdom or higher guidance from Spirit. It enables you to access the subconscious mind and receive answers to questions, especially when you feel you do not have any!

Asandra, author of *Contact Your Spirit Guides*, is a renowned US trans medium, or trans channel, who helps clients connect with their Master Guides. In her aforementioned book she writes: "Allowing the energy to flow through you requires a receptive state of being. This is why any form of meditation, prayer, visualization, etc., can only enhance the process. There is an attunement between the sender (the Spirit), and the receiver (the Channel), that must occur. Working with our Spirit Guides is a two-way communication. Only when you are open to this higher guidance, can you perceive its existence in your life. You cannot expect Spirit to be able to reach you unless you are making an effort to be open, and in contact with them."

Allow yourself the time and space to expand your aura and open your energy field (see Chapter Three). Make

an effort to practice at the same time each day or week, and make sure you are not interrupted. Practicing at the same time allows you to form a habit, and teaches your brain what is expected of it. Relax your mind by taking a few long breaths, and then return to your natural breathing rhythm.

Write down a question to help you focus your thoughts. Then let go of any expectations in order to let your experience unfold. At first, you may appear to be making things up – this is natural, especially if you are doubting your abilities. So, think of it as flushing an old rusted radiator! The rubbish will come out first, and then your channel will clear as you train your brain to be receptive and relaxed.

Asking one question per session gives you the opportunity to keep track of information you are

receiving. Very often, a specific subject, idea or type of knowledge builds over several sessions. Allow this knowledge to flow through you as you observe in a passive relaxed state. It is critical that you do not overthink what you are writing at this stage. If you notice your mind wandering away from what you're writing, gently pull your pen away from the page and use meditative techniques to re-enter the trance-like state.

Writing long-hand, with a pen on paper, is a good way to begin channelling. This causes your mind to shift to a slower mind wave, allowing information to flow more easily. Once you've mastered this technique, you'll be able to move on to typing.

When you feel that information has stopped flowing through you:

• Keep pen on paper.

• Keep writing what you are feeling. For example, "I do not know what to write now, nothing is coming through... my nose itches..." etc.

• Start making loops, but keep pen on paper.

When the logical side of your brain perceives that you are not threatened by beginning a new activity, it stops fighting it, and the writing resumes. It is also important to note that you will receive information based on the level of your vibration, which is determined by your level of personal awareness. As your energy field vibrates at a higher level, your channelling will become more profound. So stay curious, delve into subjects and interests you might not normally be interested in, and

discover your creative hobby or talent, for example.
Continue developing yourself as a person.

Here are a few simple but effective exercises to help you
develop your intuition.

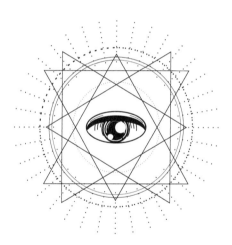

BALANCING THE BRAIN'S HEMISPHERES

Are you a right-brained or a left-brained person? The facts show that it makes no difference! According to *Medical News Today*, while each of our hemispheres serves slightly different functions, individuals do not have a 'dominant' brain side that governs their personality and abilities. We use both brain hemispheres almost equally, and all of the time.

Depending on what activity or task you are engaged in, the left hemisphere of the brain is more concerned with the use of language, while the right hemisphere is more concerned with the subtleties of nonverbal communication. In general, the left hemisphere is in charge of linear, logical, practical learning. The right hemisphere is in charge of non-linear, intuitive or abstract learning. When it comes to learning something new, there are many exercises that can help synchronize both brain hemispheres. And here's a fun way to do it!

Try this before starting any psychic development routine.

Begin by drawing an infinity figure in your journal with your dominant hand. Go over it as closely as you can to your original drawing, until you're comfortable with it. Then, using your other hand (the weaker hand), mindfully trace over that outline while staying as close as possible to the original shape you drew with your dominant hand.

When you get the hang of it, hold the pen with both hands and go over your infinity figure. Stay close to the outline you drew earlier. The goal here is focus, NOT speed. Repeating each step about ten times improves mind-body integration and reduces cognitive anxiety. It also maximizes your brain's ability by syncing both halves in a short time.

CANDLE FLAME

Candles have long been connected with spiritual pursuits, making them an ideal medium for activating your psychic channel. Staring at a candle has a calming effect, as you contemplate the flickering flame. It helps you focus your mind on the present moment, leaving other thoughts behind. When you want to relax, open your psychic channel or meditate, you might want to develop a ritual of lighting a tea-light candle if you enjoyed this exercise.

As you light the candle, state an intention in your mind, contemplate it, or simply relax your focus, keeping your eyes on the flame. Allow your thoughts to drift as you wonder at the beauty of the flame – its shape or colour, for instance.

Stay as long as you like, or until the flame goes out. A tea-light candle is generally best, as you do not want to fall asleep and risk a fire hazard! If you begin to feel too comfortable and relaxed, please extinguish the flame and rest.

As you extinguish the flame, you can either reaffirm
your intention, give thanks for being guided or simply
say "*from light to light*", confirming your connection to
higher wisdom. Remember that intuition frequently
emerges after relaxation. So, if you are not too sleepy,
now is the ideal time jot down any thoughts, ideas or
inspiration that popped into your head as your thoughts
blended with the flame. Otherwise, rest or go to sleep.
You may even generate an enlightening dream!

TREES

Communicating with other energy fields is another
delightful technique to activate your intuition. To
begin with, you may find it simpler to tune in to 'living'
energy fields, such as those of trees. As you become
more comfortable with it, practice communicating with
energy fields of animals, birds or flowers, and ultimately
progress towards inanimate objects or faraway locations.
The sky is the literal limit.

Do you remember Figure 4: Communication between
energy fields, in Chapter Three? Locate your favourite
tree, such as one in a garden or a park. In your mind,
ask for permission to 'enter' the space of that tree.
Walk mindfully towards the tree, thanking it for its
permission, and place your palms on the tree's trunk.
Relax as you breathe, and allow the information to flow
to you effortlessly (do not strain).

To receive information, it helps to ask questions –
especially when it comes to intuitive communication.
Try asking the tree in your mind if it is female, male
or non-binary. Communication between two energy
fields can be instant. Energy reacts instantly, making it
easier to start receiving responses or impressions. "Are
you older or younger?" is another example to keep the
conversation going. "What would you do if you had a
job?" is another.

Relax and let go of any expectations while your palms pick up any sensations or information. Because everyone is unique, you may see impressions with your third eye, receive answers as ideas in your head, or simply experience a different vibration through your palms. If you do this exercise with a friend, it becomes even more interesting.

Try to talk to three trees, and practice communicating with each one simultaneously with your friend. Record your impressions if you need to, before you compare your information with your friend. When you have each finished, sit down and compare the information you received independently. You might just astound yourselves!

On Your Psychic Journey

Finally, remember that you are your greatest asset
and the catalyst of your own growth when it comes
to developing your psychic potential. The path of
awakening your intuition is more important than the
destination:

- Know that your brain is already wired for psychic
  perception.

- Pay attention to your common sense and stay
  attentive and interested in exploring new areas.

- Rather than experiencing phenomena, seek to develop
  excellent results – the former merely feeds your ego.
  So, anything you are inspired with will be far from
  originating from the highest source, or for your
  highest good.

- Take care of your instrument. "Human beings are walking batteries," according to physicist and geomancer Dr. Jude Currivan. Psychic messages are neuro-electrical pulses travelling to and from your brain. Make sure you eat healthily, stay hydrated and get plenty of rest.

- Discover your own rhythm. Allow yourself time to recuperate and integrate the experiences you have had before applying the wisdom of what you have learned. Go at your own pace to allow your gifts to unfold naturally and safely.

- Set a time when you can practice consistently and systematically. Create your own ideal strategy and rituals to help you, such as lighting a tea-light candle or burning incense before you begin.

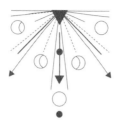

- All information you perceive through your conventional senses, as well as throughout your body, is processed by your brain. This is linked to your spine, through which all information is routed to your brain. So, when training, remember to sit comfortably or lie down with your back flat and rested. Information will travel more easily!

- Your psychic gifts are to empower and inspire you and possibly loved ones around you. Please keep regular notes to steer your psychic path, note what aspects you prefer, and develop each as far and as best as you can before moving on to the next. They are there to inspire, not to manipulate or sow doubt. Be accountable.

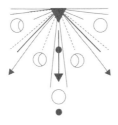

- When you begin any psychic session, set your intention, ask for protection, ask to be guided for your highest good (or find your own words), and ask to be replenished at the end. Return to your body, your conventional senses, and your normal life after that, grateful for being supported and inspired with insights.

Whatever you choose to do with your psychic abilities, try not to bring negativity into the minds of others or yourself. The term 'inspiration' is derived from the word 'spirit'. Intuitive communications are joyful, encouraging, compassionate and wise.